h to

# *Teach Speaking*

## Scott Thornbury

Longman

series editor:
Jeremy Harmer

# Contents

# Introduction

**Who is this book for?**

*How to Teach Speaking* has been written for all teachers of English who wish to improve their knowledge and to develop their classroom skills in this important area.

**What is this book about?**

It is generally accepted that knowing a language and being able to speak it are not synonymous. Thus, the claim *She knows Italian* does not entail the statement *She can speak Italian*. Yet, in many ways, the teaching of second or other languages has carried on as if knowing and speaking were the same thing. That is, you learn the grammar and you learn some vocabulary and you make sentences which you pronounce properly, and hey presto, you can speak! This is reflected in generations of books on oral English, which are essentially just books on how to vocalize grammar.

Research – and common sense – suggests that there is a lot more to speaking than the ability to form grammatically correct sentences and then to pronounce them. For a start, speaking is interactive and requires the ability to co-operate in the management of speaking turns. It also typically takes place in real time, with little time for detailed planning. In these circumstances, spoken fluency requires the capacity to marshal a store of memorized lexical chunks. And the nature of the speaking process means that the grammar of spoken language differs in a number of significant ways from the grammar of written language. Hence, the study of written grammar may not be the most efficient preparation for speaking.

No wonder speaking represents a real challenge to most language learners. Speaking is a skill, and as such needs to be developed and practised independently of the grammar curriculum. This book, therefore, attempts to redress the lack of available guides to the teaching of 'speaking-as-skill'. Accordingly, in Chapter 1 we start by looking at what skilled speakers can do before looking at what they know (in Chapter 2). Chapter 3 addresses the problems faced by speakers of another language and maps out a number of priorities for the teaching of speaking. The succeeding three chapters deal with the three stages of a general approach to skill-development: awareness-raising (Chapter 4), appropriation (Chapter 5), and autonomy (Chapter 6). Finally, in Chapter 7, we look at ways that speaking can be integrated into the language curriculum and at some approaches to its assessment.

Practical classroom applications are signalled throughout by this icon 🎙. Finally, the Task File consists of photocopiable task sheets, relevant to each chapter. They can be used for individual study and reflection or for discussion and review in a training context. An answer key is provided. This is followed by chapter notes and further reading suggestions. The source information for the extracts within the chapters is provided in the chapter notes.

# 1 What speakers do

- Introduction
- Speech production
- Conceptualization and formulation
- Articulation
- Self-monitoring and repair
- Automaticity
- Fluency
- Managing talk

**Introduction**

> 'My students always say that they want more speaking, but I don't know how to teach it, apart from giving them lots of useful expressions.'
>
> 'I've been asked to teach a conversation class, but what is conversation? Is it just free speaking?'
>
> 'How much grammar do students need before they can have conversations?'
>
> 'How can I help my students become more fluent? What is fluency? Is it good pronunciation?'
>
> 'My business students are good at giving presentations, but they can't have even the simplest conversations. How can I help them improve?'

Questions like these – from a teachers' on-line discussion forum – may be familiar to you. They express some of the common dilemmas teachers face when trying to address the teaching of speaking. For a long time it was assumed that the ability to speak fluently followed naturally from the teaching of grammar and vocabulary, with a bit of pronunciation thrown in. We now know that speaking is much more complex than this and that it involves both a command of certain skills and several different types of knowledge. In this chapter we will look at speaking from the first of these perspectives: what is it that good speakers *can do*? In the chapter that follows we will address the second question: what is it that good speakers know?

**Speech production**

Speaking is so much a part of daily life that we take it for granted. The average person produces tens of thousands of words a day, although some people – like auctioneers or politicians – may produce even more than that. So natural and integral is speaking that we forget how we once struggled to achieve this ability – until, that is, we have to learn how to do it all over again in a foreign language.

What then is involved in speaking? The first point to emphasize is that speech production takes place in real time and is therefore essentially **linear**. Words follow words, and phrases follow phrases. Likewise, at the level of **utterance** (that is to say, the spoken equivalent of sentences), speech is produced utterance-by-utterance, in response to the word-by-word and utterance-by-utterance productions of the person we are talking to (our **interlocutor**). This **contingent** nature of speech, whereby each utterance is dependent on a preceding one, accounts for its **spontaneity**. This is not to say that speech is unplanned, only that the planning time is severely limited. And the planning of one utterance may overlap with the production of the previous one. These 'real-time processing' demands of speech production explain many of the characteristics of spoken language.

In the following extract from a dinner party conversation about traditional British foods (which we will call *Kedgeree*, after the fish dish it names, for ease of reference) we can get a sense of speech production in operation. There are five speakers, and the subject of *junket* (an English milky dessert) has come up. One of the speakers, Kath, then says:

| | | |
|---|---|---|
| (1) | Kath: | I made junket when I was in the first year of secondary school. |

(The numeral (1) is the way speaker **turns** are usually indicated in transcriptions. A **turn** is the duration of one speaker's contribution to the talk before yielding to, or being interrupted by, another speaker). Other transcription conventions are:

=   contiguous utterances, i.e. ones that run on without pause, despite interruptions from other speakers
|   overlapping utterances
‖   simultaneous utterances
( )  a slip

The conversation about junket meanders on, until 51 turns later Kath says:

| | | |
|---|---|---|
| (52) | Kath: | It's one of those ridiculously old-fashioned dishes that they make you cook in domestic science = |
| (53) | Hilda: | This is really nice this Rioja |
| (54) | Nick: | Well why don't you try making ǀsome? Might be great |
| (55) | Kath: | ǀ= like kedgeree |
| (56) | Simon: | Spotted dick. |
| (57) | Kath: | = Kedgeree, I remember saying to my mum = |
| (58) | Scott: | Toad-in-the-hole |
| (59) | Kath: | = I've got to take a pound of fish next week we're making kedgeree and she said [mock accent] 'you don't want to be making kedgeree' [laughter] and she said 'we don't like it'. And I had to take a note to my domestic science (taitch-) teacher saying 'Kathleen can't make kedgeree because we don't like it'. [laughter] Awful. So I couldn't make it. I had to sit there while everybody else did. [laughter]. |

Continues ...

| (60) Hilda: | I would just make egg and bacon |
|---|---|
| (61) Kath: | But kedgeree. This was a sort of comprehensive school the first year of. Nobody knew what kedgeree was. It was sort of kedgeree and junket [laughter] |
| (62) Simon: | ‖ I love kedgeree |
| (63) Kath: | ‖ I mean for God's sake |
| (64) Simon: | Have you ever eaten kedgeree since? |
| (65) Kath: | ‖ Oh yes I love kedgeree |
| (66) Nick: | ‖ Didn't you say you could get hold of a decent bloody |
| (67) Kath: | It's a sort of old colonial dish = |
| (68) Simon: | = It is yes it's Indian |
| (69) Kath: | = like junket is but it was so ∣ inappropriate = |
| (70) Nick: | ∣ oh is it like galub jalum? |
| (71) Kath: | = for the first year comprehensive school kids to be making [laughs]. |

**Conceptualization and formulation**

The mention of *junket* seems to have triggered an association in Kath's mind with domestic science classes (turn 1), which in turn reminds her of a story about – not junket – but kedgeree. At some point (it may have been at the initial mention of *junket*) she **conceptualizes** the story – in terms of its discourse type (*a story*), its topic (*kedgeree*), and its purpose (*to amuse*). She then has to wait for the appropriate moment to re-introduce it (turns 52 and 55), where she adroitly shifts the topic from *junket* to *kedgeree*. Finally, at turn 57, she is able to 'gain the floor' and is ready to tell her story.

But first the story-idea has to be mapped out, or **formulated**. This involves making strategic choices at the level of discourse, syntax, and vocabulary. At the level of overall discourse, stories have a typical structure, or **script**. At the very least, they have a beginning, middle, and end. Discourse scripts are part of our shared background knowledge, and can be 'pulled down off the shelf', as it were, thereby saving formulation time, while also easing the load of the listener, who quickly recognizes what script has been selected.

Each of the stages of the script then needs to be fleshed out at the utterance level. This is where the specific **syntax** of each utterance needs to be chosen so that the content of the story is packaged in a way that is consistent with the speaker's intentions. Initially, this will mean deciding on what elements of the utterance will go in what order. In English, utterances tend to have a two-part structure: the first part is the **topic**, i.e. what we are talking about, and the second part is the **comment**, i.e. what we want to say about the topic. So, in Kath's turn 67: *It's a sort of old colonial dish*, the topic is *it* (referring to the previously mentioned *kedgeree*) and the comment is everything that follows:

| topic | comment |
|---|---|
| It [kedgeree] | is a sort of old colonial dish. |

The topic is typically information that has already been mentioned (**given information**), while the comment is usually something new.

The 'grammaring' of each utterance is also constrained by how much information can be held in working memory at any one time. One way speakers compensate for limited planning time is to use what is called an **add-on strategy**. This is the chaining together of short phrases and clause-like chunks, which accumulate to form an extended turn. We can see the add-on strategy operating in Kath's turn 61 in the Kedgeree conversation. Each stage in the sequence is marked with a vertical line:

> But kedgeree.| This was a sort of comprehensive school | the first year of.| Nobody knew what kedgeree was.| It was sort of kedgeree and junket

If this had been a written sentence, it would probably have been constructed quite differently, with more embedding (or **subordination**) of components, rather than simply chaining them together. (See page 53 for an example of how this might be done.) This accounts for the often fragmented appearance of spoken language when it is transcribed. In listening to spoken language we tend to 'iron out' its creases, so that we hear it as a smooth continuum.

Having 'laid out' the utterance in terms of its syntactic elements, the speaker now needs to assign individual words or phrases to the different 'slots' in the layout. Take, for example, Kath's decision (in turn 57) to use the words *my mum* to fill the slot at the end of *I remember saying to … .* Kath's choice of the word *mum* rather than *mother*, for example, may be due to the fact that she uses this term more frequently when talking about this person. On the other hand, the choice may be determined by an assessment of how appropriate the word is for the particular context. For the purposes of the anecdote that Kath is telling, which pokes gentle fun at her mother, the more informal *mum* probably felt more appropriate.

When a wrong word is accessed, it will usually be a word – or combination of words – that is similar in meaning or form, or both, to the targeted word. Production slips often occur when speakers are under pressure or tired. Sports commentators, for example, are particularly susceptible to this, and collections of sporting gaffes circulate freely on the Internet. For example:

> 'I can see the carrot at the end of the tunnel.' (Stuart Pearce)
> 'The tackles are coming in thick and thin.' (Alan Brazil, on Radio 5 Live)
> 'Barnsley have started off the way they mean to begin.' (Chris Kamara)

At some stage, the words need to be 'glued together' by the insertion of the appropriate grammatical markers, such as articles (*the*, *a* etc), auxiliary verbs (*is*, *did*, *have* etc) and word endings (*-ing*, *-er*, *-ed*, and so on). Occasionally, even native speakers make slips at this level, producing *I buyed it* for *I bought it*, for example, although they are always quick to correct these slips.

Also at the formulation stage, the words need to be assigned their pronunciation. This will include not only the individual sounds of the words but the appropriate placement of prominence (**stress**) and the meaningful use of **intonation** (pitch direction). Because sentence stress and intonation are implicated in the way new or important information is signalled, it is likely that choices at this level have been made at the initial 'laying out' stage. So, when Simon asks (in turn 64) *Have you ever eaten kedgeree since?*, the key piece of new information is not *kedgeree*, which has already been mentioned, but the last word, *since*. This is therefore given extra prominence. Also, because he's asking a *yes/no* question, the pitch direction rises on the word *since*. In Kath's reply (turn 65), prominence is given to the word *love*: *Oh yes I LOVE kedgeree*, and the direction of pitch change is down, conveying the completion of the idea posed by Simon's question.

**Articulation**     What has been formulated now needs to be articulated. Articulation involves the use of the organs of speech to produce sounds. A stream of air is produced in the lungs, driven through the vocal cords, and 'shaped' by, among other things, the position and movement of the tongue, teeth, and lips. Vowel sounds are produced primarily by the action of the tongue and the lips. Consonant sounds are determined by the point at which the air stream is obstructed − e.g. at the lips or teeth − and the kind of constriction the air stream is subjected to, e.g. whether it is made to 'pop' or to 'buzz'.

The combined effect of all these variables allows speakers of English to produce a range of over 40 **phonemes**, i.e. sounds that, in English, determine the meaning of a word. These are divided almost equally between vowels and consonants: the exact number will vary according to the variety of English spoken. (For a fuller description, see *How to Teach Pronunciation* by Gerald Kelly.)

The rather oversimplified account, above, might suggest that individual sounds are produced one at a time, in the manner of a sausage-machine. In fact, sounds are produced in a continuous stream, with many different vocal organs involved concurrently, such that the articulation of one sound will affect the articulation of its neighbours. This accounts for the way, in fluent speech, some sounds merge with other sounds (as in the way *handbag* sounds like *hambag*) or are dropped completely, as is the final *d* in *baked beans*.

At the same time as these articulatory processes are engaged, continual changes in loudness, pitch direction, tempo, and pausing serve to organize the sounds into meaningful word forms, and the words into meaningful utterances. All this physical work happens, of course, at great speed. It is estimated that proficient speakers produce 15 phonemes a second. Sometimes, in the rush to speak, interference from neighbouring words causes pronunciation slips, as when Kath says (turn 59): *And I had to take a note to my domestic science taitch- teacher saying … .* Here, her anticipation of the /eɪ/ sound in *saying* seems to have interfered with the correct pronunciation of *teacher*, which she starts to pronounce as *taitcher*.

**Self-monitoring and repair**     This quick self-correction of Kath's is an instance of **self-monitoring**, a process that happens concurrently with the stages of conceptualization, formulation, and articulation. A re-think at the planning stage may result in the abandonment of the message altogether, as when someone starts to gossip and then realizes that the subject of the gossip is within hearing distance! Self-monitoring at the formulation stage may result in a slowing down, or a pause and the subsequent backtracking and re-phrasing of an utterance. Self-monitoring of articulation results in the kind of corrections that even fluent speakers have to make when the wrong word pops out or the pronunciation goes awry.

Hand in hand with monitoring is the ability to make running **repairs**, either in response to self-monitoring or to the messages conveyed by one's interlocutors. Repair can take the form of an immediate correction (as in Kath's *taitch-* to *teacher*) or 'retrace-and-repair' sequences, that is, when the speaker retraces or 're-winds' an utterance, and starts again, but with a different sequence of words or phrases, as in:

> Dad, I don't think you sh-, I think you should leave Chris home Saturday.

**Automaticity**

All this conceptualizing, formulating, articulating, and monitoring mean that a speaker's attentional resources are very thinly stretched. In order to achieve any degree of fluency, therefore, some degree of **automaticity** is necessary. Automaticity allows speakers to focus their attention on the aspect of the speaking task that immediately requires it, whether it is planning or articulation.

At the level of formulation, automaticity is partly achieved through the use of **prefabricated chunks**. Kath saves valuable planning time by using expressions like *I remember + -ing*, as in *I remember saying to my mum … .* This is an instance of a chunk that acts as a kind of springboard into the anecdote that follows, one that is commonly used to introduce anecdotes. The repeated linking device *and she said* is another instance of a ready-made unit that is common in storytelling.

At the discourse level, a degree of automaticity is possible too. Kath's story is told with little hesitation and no false starts probably because she has told this story a number of times before. Not only is the overall design of the story familiar to her, but whole segments of it (such as *'Kathleen can't make kedgeree because we don't like it'*) may have been memorized from previous tellings.

In this sense, speaking is like any other skill, such as driving or playing a musical instrument: the more practice you get, the more likely it is you will be able to chunk small units into larger ones. With fewer units to assemble at the moment of articulation, there is a proportionally greater gain in fluency. Conversely, embarking on a completely untried speech genre, on an unfamiliar topic, with unknown interlocutors, is likely to make one 'tongue-tied' at best, or, at worst, completely mute. Wilbur Wright, writing of his first ventures in aeronautics, said, 'Skill comes by the constant repetition of familiar feats rather than by a few over-bold attempts at feats for which the performer is yet poorly prepared.' The same could be said for spoken fluency.

**Fluency**

What exactly is **fluency**, then? When we talk about someone as being 'a fluent speaker of French' or when we say 'she speaks the language fluently', what do we mean? Is fluency simply the ability to speak fast? Speed *is* a factor, but it is by no means the only – or even the most important – one. Research into listeners' perceptions of a speaker's fluency suggests that **pausing** is equally important. All speakers pause – they have to, to draw breath. And even proficient speakers need to stop from time to time to allow the formulation of an utterance to catch up with its conceptualization. But frequent pausing is a sure sign of a struggling speaker. If the speaker – produces – one – word – at – a – time – like – this – no matter how accurate the results are, the speaker will not normally be judged a fluent speaker. In fact, in terms of how listeners rate a speaker's fluency, the frequency of pausing is more significant than the length of the pauses.

Also important is the appropriate **placement** of pauses. Natural-sounding pauses | are those that occur at the intersection of clauses, |or after groups of words that form a meaningful unit.| (The vertical lines in the last sentence mark where natural pauses might occur if the sentence were being spoken.) Unnatural | pauses, on the | other hand, occur | midway between related groups of | words.

Another significant factor in the perception of fluency is the length of run, i.e. the number of syllables between pauses. The longer the runs, the more fluent the speaker sounds. Studies of speakers who are 'abnormally fluent', such as auctioneers and horse-race commentators, show that such speakers hardly ever hesitate or backtrack, and take only minimal pauses for breath. Moreover, the runs between these pauses are enormous. Here is an example of a single run in a New Zealand race-caller's live commentary:

> They're off and racing now and one of the best out was Speedy Cheval coming out at number two from El Red and also Florlis Fella's away fairly well, a little wider on the track the favourite Race Ruler, Twilight Time is in behind those.

Researchers found that the race-caller's fluency was due in large part to the fact that, rather than constructing each utterance from scratch, he was using prefabricated chunks – sequences he had memorized through constant practice.

Race-callers and auctioneers are, of course, somewhat exceptional. Nevertheless, we all know someone of whom it is said 'you can't get a word in edgeways', just as we have all experienced the sensation ourselves of being totally 'tongue-tied'. Somewhere in between is the notion of normal fluency.

In order to give at least the illusion of fluency and to compensate for the attentional demands involved in speech production, speakers use a number of 'tricks' – or **production strategies**. One of them is the ability to disguise pauses by filling them. The most common **pause fillers** are *uh* and *um* (also spelt *er* and *erm*, respectively). Some **vagueness** expressions, like *sort of* and *I mean* are also used to fill pauses. Another common device for gaining formulation time is the use of **repeats** – that is the repetition of a single word at the point where formulation has been temporarily paused. In this short extract, the speaker uses both fillers and repeats (the dot indicates a short pause):

> well what's the · what's the failure with the football I mean this · this I don't really see I mean it · cos the money · how much does it cost to get in down the road now?

The features of fluency can now be summarized:

- pauses may be long but not frequent.
- pauses are usually filled.
- pauses occur at meaningful transition points.
- there are long runs of syllables and words between pauses.

## Managing talk

### Interaction

So far we have been describing what speakers do as if they were speaking in a kind of vacuum, but of course most speaking takes the form of face-to-face dialogue and therefore involves interaction. Even in monologic speaking, such as lectures, political speeches, and stand-up comedy, most speakers adjust their delivery to take into account the response of their audience. In the Kedgeree conversation, for example, we saw how Kath had to work hard, conversationally speaking, both to gain the floor and to switch the topic so that she could tell her story:

| | |
|---|---|
| (52) Kath: | It's one of those ridiculously old-fashioned dishes that they make you cook in domestic science = |
| (53) Hilda: | This is really nice this Rioja |
| (54) Nick: | Well why don't you try making ǀ some? Might be great |
| (55) Kath: | ǀ = like kedgeree |
| (56) Simon: | Spotted dick. |
| (57) Kath: | = Kedgeree, I remember saying to my mum = |
| (58) Scott: | Toad-in-the-hole |
| (59) Kath: | = I've got to take a pound of fish next week we're making kedgeree … |

Notice how other speakers are jockeying for conversational turns, introducing new topics and engaging in word play (naming old-fashioned dishes with comical names) and that this causes a certain amount of overlapping (i.e. more than one speaker speaking at once) and lack of coherence. But once Kath has wrested the topic and the floor, the others sit back and listen, recognizing that she has embarked on an anecdote.

### Turn-taking

This delicate moment is successfully negotiated because the speakers are familiar with the rules and skills of **turn-taking**. The fundamental rule of turn-taking is:

- speakers should take turns to hold the floor.

This implies that no two speakers should be speaking at once, at least not for any sustained period of time. There are two further rules, although the first of these is arguably culturally specific:

- long silences are to be avoided.
- listen when other speakers are speaking.

The skills by means of which these rules are observed include:

- recognizing the appropriate moment to get a turn.
- signalling the fact that you want to speak.
- holding the floor while you have your turn.
- recognizing when other speakers are signalling their wish to speak.
- yielding the turn.
- signalling the fact that you are listening.

In some contexts, such as in a business meeting or a classroom, these interactional moves are formally signalled by, for example, the raising of one's hand. In casual talk between friends, however, it is largely the use of **discourse markers** that signals a speaker's conversational intentions. A discourse marker is to speaking what a car's indicator lights are to driving: it lets other speakers know what your intentions are. Typical discourse markers for managing turn-taking include:

*that reminds me* (= I'm continuing the same topic)
*by the way* (= I'm indicating a topic change)
*well anyway* (= I'm returning to the topic)
*like I say* (= I'm repeating what I said before)
*yes, but* (= I'm indicating a difference of opinion)
*yes no I know* (= I'm indicating agreement with a negative idea)
*uh-huh* (= I'm listening)

Strictly speaking, *uh-huh* is not a discourse marker but a **backchannel device**, i.e. a means of signalling to your interlocutor that you are listening, and, in the case of *really?* and *no!*, not only listening, but interested, shocked etc.

### Paralinguistics

Negotiation of speaking turns does not rely on words alone. A sharp intake of breath and a raising of the shoulders, for example, signal the wish to take a turn. At the same time, the speaker-to-be typically glances away from the current speaker: it's not customary to start talking when looking directly at your interlocutor. During a speaking turn, little head nods from listeners tend to encourage speakers to speak faster, but if someone stands with their arms crossed, most speakers slow down. As speakers approach the end of their turn, there is a tendency to let the shoulders fall, and to re-direct their gaze back at their interlocutors, as if to say 'I've done'. The interactional use of eye gaze and gesture are known as **paralinguistics**. Of course, these paralinguistic signals apply only in face-to-face conversation. When speaking on the phone, listeners have to rely on other means, such as intonation, tempo, and pausing, to gauge the current state of their interlocutor's turn.

**Conclusions**    In this opening chapter we've tried to get 'inside the head' of a language speaker. What exactly happens when thoughts become utterances? We noted that speaking consists of at least three stages:

- conceptualization
- formulation
- articulation

during which the speaker is also engaged in:

- self-monitoring

Speakers achieve fluency because these processes are, to some extent, automated. The use of production strategies, such as the filling of pauses, also contributes to fluency. At the same time as they are speaking, speakers are also having to gauge the effect they are having on their interlocutors, as well as to take into account the contributions other speakers are making to the talk, both linguistic and paralinguistic. This involves an ability to manage turn-taking.

**Looking ahead**     So far, we have looked at the mental and physiological processes implicated in speaking. But what does a speaker need to *know*, in order that these processes are optimally realized? That is the subject of the next chapter.

# 2 What speakers know

- **Extralinguistic knowledge**
  - o **Sociocultural knowledge**
- **Linguistic knowledge**
  - o **Genre knowledge**
  - o **Discourse knowledge**
  - o **Pragmatic knowledge**
  - o **Grammar**
  - o **Vocabulary**
  - o **Phonology**
- **Speech conditions**

In the last chapter we treated speaking as a **skill**, in the same way you might talk about the skill of playing the guitar or of driving a car. But being *skilful* assumes having some kind of knowledge base. To play a guitar well requires some kind of musical knowledge; to drive a car requires knowing something about how it works, as well as knowing the highway code. Of course, the knowledge base for speaking in a first language is largely intuitive; it is not something a person is normally sufficiently aware of to be able to describe. In order to describe it, researchers are compelled to infer it, both from the evidence of actual performance and also by studying the way it develops in early childhood. We shall draw on that evidence to identify what it is that speakers *know*. Knowledge that is relevant to speaking can be categorized either as knowledge of features of language (**linguistic knowledge**) or knowledge that is independent of language (**extralinguistic knowledge**).

**Extralinguistic knowledge**  The kinds of extralinguistic knowledge that affect speaking include such things as topic and cultural knowledge, knowledge of the context, and familiarity with the other speakers. In the dinner-party conversation about kedgeree (page 2), the speakers share considerable background knowledge at all these levels, and this is reflected in the assumptions they are able to make. Kath, for example, doesn't have to explain what *domestic science* is, and the other speakers throw in references to *spotted dick*, *toad-in-the-hole*, and *galub jalum*, as if these concepts were part of their common experience. These all constitute topic and cultural knowledge.

Context knowledge allows speakers to make reference to the immediate context, as in Hilda's mention of *this Rioja* (referring to the wine they are drinking). The use of mild oaths, such as *I mean for God's sake* (turn 63), suggests that, in this conversation, there is a level of interpersonal familiarity between the speakers that permits a degree of informality that would not be the case with total strangers.

Of course not all speaking events can rely on quite such a degree of shared knowledge. Explaining street directions to a total stranger or giving a lecture on quantum theory are both uses of speech that will require a considerable degree of explicitness. But because most speaking takes place face to face, and in a shared context, there is generally less need to be as explicit as one might normally be in writing, for example. After all, if your interlocutors don't understand you, they only have to ask. This 'situated' nature of speech means that it is characteristically *elliptic*: i.e. words, phrases, whole clauses are left out because they are redundant. So, when Hilda, in turn 60, says: *I would just make egg and bacon*, what is understood is the unstated idea: *... when I did domestic science at school*.

Other characteristics of spoken language that derive from its being grounded in a shared context are:

- high frequency of personal pronouns, especially *you* and *I*;
- the use of substitute forms, as in (turn 59) *I had to sit there while everybody else did*, where *did* substitutes for *made kedgeree*;
- and the use of **deictic** language, that is, words or expressions that make direct reference to the context, as in *this Rioja*.

### Sociocultural knowledge

*'In X country long silences are tolerated in conversations.'*
*'In Y country you don't normally ask people why they are not married.'*
*'In Z country you always refuse an offer at least three times before accepting.'*

Statements like these belong to the area of **sociocultural knowledge**. This is knowledge about social values and the norms of behaviour in a given society, including the way these values and norms are realized through language. Sociocultural knowledge can be both extralinguistic and linguistic. Knowing whether people in a given culture shake hands on meeting, or embrace, or bow, is extralinguistic; knowing what they say when they greet each other is clearly linguistic.

There has been a lot of debate as to the extent to which cultural differences cause misunderstandings or even breakdowns in communication. Unfortunately, the topic gives rise to a great deal of 'folk theorizing' and cultural stereotyping, of the type *All Japanese do such-and-such* and *All Arabs say so-and-so ...* . In fact, studies of conversational style suggest that there may be as many differences *within* a particular culture as there are between cultures. In any group of talkers anywhere, there is always someone who will dominate the conversation and someone else who won't say very much at all.

Nevertheless, there are certain speech events, such as greetings, requests, or apologies, where the risk of causing offence has meant that these events have become ritualized in different ways across social groups. Part of a speaker's knowledge, then, is knowing what these sociocultural rules are and how they are codified.

**Linguistic knowledge**

Linguistic knowledge is often ranged along a cline from 'the big picture', e.g. knowledge of the way an anecdote typically unfolds, to the 'fine print', e.g. knowledge of grammar and vocabulary. In fact, the boundaries between categories are blurred, and they work interdependently, such that in reality it is difficult to account for particular features of a speech event by reference to any single knowledge system. However, for convenience, we shall discuss these different levels in turn.

### Genre knowledge

Very broadly, there are two main purposes for speaking. Speaking serves either a **transactional** function, in that its primary purpose is to convey information and facilitate the exchange of goods or services, or it serves an **interpersonal** function, in that its primary purpose is to establish and maintain social relations. A typical transactional speech event might be phoning to book a table at a restaurant. A typical interpersonal speech event might be the conversation between friends that takes place *at* the restaurant. The story that Kath tells about her domestic science class is motivated less by the need to convey the facts of the matter (i.e. a transactional purpose) than by the wish to amuse her audience and thereby maintain a sense of shared community between friends (i.e. an interpersonal purpose).

These two basic purposes for speaking generate a host of different types of speech events. These, in turn, will be sequenced and structured in accordance with the kinds of social and mental processes that they accompany. We saw, for example, how Kath told her kedgeree story according to a narrative **script**, which, to put it very simply, has a beginning, middle, and end.

**Service encounters**, such as buying goods, getting information, or requesting a service, are transactional speech events that follow a fairly predictable script. Typically, the exchange begins with a greeting, followed by an offer, followed by a request, and so on, as in:

> Good morning.
> Good morning.
> What would you like?
> A dozen eggs, please.
> Anything else? …
> etc.

A certain amount of variation is generally permitted: some of the moves may be dispensable, while others of a more interpersonal nature – such as a comment about the weather – might be optional. Different cultures and sub-cultures may develop their own variants. Some service encounters in some cultures may permit bargaining, for example.

Over time and within particular speech communities, certain ways of realizing these speech events have become conventionalized to the point that they have evolved into specific **genres**. Genre is an elusive term. Here we will use it to mean simply a type of speech event, especially in terms of how that speech event might be labelled by its participants. Hence, there is a difference between saying 'I had a chat with the boss' and 'I had a job interview with the boss' or 'I did a presentation to the boss'. Knowledge of how specific genres – such as chatting, job interviews, or business presentations – are realized is part of the linguistic knowledge that speakers in a particular speech community share. (How genres are integrated into genre-based teaching programmes is discussed in Chapter 7.)

An important factor that determines the structure of a genre is whether it is **interactive** or **non-interactive**. Multi-party speech, as in a shopping exchange or casual conversation between friends, is jointly constructed and interactive. Monologues, such as a television journalist's live report, a university lecture, or when you leave a voice-mail message, are non-interactive.

Finally, a distinction needs to be made between **planned** and **unplanned** speech. Certain speech genres, such as public speeches and business presentations, are typically planned, to the point that they might be completely scripted in advance. This means that their linguistic features will resemble or replicate features of written language. On the other hand, a phone conversation to ask for train timetable information, while following a predictable sequence, is normally not planned in advance: each participant has to make strategic and spontaneous decisions on the basis of the way the discourse unfolds. This, in turn, will affect the kind of language used.

On the basis of these criteria, we can classify speaking genres according to their general purposes, the kind of participation they involve, and the degree of planning (bearing in mind that these distinctions are less polarities than stages on a continuum). For example:

| | purpose | participation | planning |
|---|---|---|---|
| airport announcements | transactional | non-interactive | planned |
| sports commentary | transactional | non-interactive | unplanned |
| job interview | transactional | interactive | (partly) planned |
| service encounter | transactional | interactive | unplanned |
| joke telling | interpersonal | (partly) interactive | (partly) planned |
| leaving a voice-mail message | transactional or interpersonal | non-interactive | unplanned |
| casual conversation | interpersonal | interactive | unplanned |

### Discourse knowledge

Within the structure of a specific genre, its individual elements need to be connected so as to form coherent stretches of discourse. Knowing how to organize and connect individual utterances, as well as how to map this knowledge on to the turn-taking structures of interactive talk, is called **discourse competence**. For example, when Kath says:

> It's one of those ridiculously old-fashioned dishes that they make you cook in domestic science

Nick responds:

> Well why don't you try making some? Might be great

His use of the **discourse marker** *Well* serves to link his utterance to Kath's previous turn, while the pronoun *some* substitutes for the previously mentioned *kedgeree*, referred to as *it* by Kath. Likewise, the ellipted *it* in Nick's utterance *might be great* also refers back to *kedgeree*. Further cohesion between the two turns is achieved through the use of the synonyms: Kath's *cook* is echoed in Nick's use of *making*. Thus, the speakers are drawing on their lexical and grammatical knowledge to make connections between utterances and across turns, within the strict constraints of the rules of turn-taking.

The use of discourse markers is particularly important in terms of the fluid management of interactive talk. Discourse markers are used to signal one's intentions, to hold the conversational turn, and to mark boundaries in the talk. For example, in the following extract Kath signals, in turn 61, that she hasn't quite relinquished the topic of kedgeree, nor drawn a moral for her story, despite Hilda's comment about egg and bacon.

| (60) | Hilda: | I would just make egg and bacon |
|---|---|---|
| (61) | Kath: | But kedgeree. This was a sort of comprehensive school the first year of. |

Kath uses the discourse marker *But* to retrieve the topic, to connect her utterance with her previous story, and to signal the contrastive nature of the conclusion she wants to draw.

Here are some common discourse markers and their meanings:

- *right, now, anyway:* these mark the beginning or closing of a segment of talk.
- *well:* this is a very common way of initiating a turn and linking it to the preceding turn, often to mark the onset of a contrast, e.g. a difference of opinion.
- *oh:* this is typically used either to launch an utterance or to respond to the previous speaker's utterance, often with implications of surprise or unexpectedness.
- *and, but, or:* these conjunctions are used to connect discourse: *and* marks some kind of continuity, *but* marks a contrast, and *or* marks an option.
- *so, because:* these are also conjunctions: they signal that what follows is (respectively) the *result* or the *cause* of what has been mentioned.
- *then:* this is often used to signal an inference based on what someone else has said.

- *y'know, I mean:* these markers serve to gain and maintain attention on the speaker – the first by appealing to the hearer's shared knowledge, and the second by signalling that some kind of clarification is going to follow.

### Pragmatic knowledge

Pragmatics describes the relation between language and its contexts of use, including the purposes for which language is being used. How do speakers adjust their message to take context into account? And how do listeners use contextual information to make sense of what they are hearing?

- **Speech acts**

  A communicative view of language holds as axiomatic that when someone says something, they are also *doing* something. For example, in the kedgeree conversation, Hilda (turn 53) says:

  > This is really nice this Rioja

  and at almost the same time Nick (turn 54) says:

  > Well why don't you try making some [kedgeree]? Might be great

  Both Hilda's and Nick's utterances have a communicative purpose: Hilda's utterance functions as praise; Nick's as a suggestion. There are both lexical and grammatical clues that help us in assigning a function to these utterances. For example, the structure *This is really X, this Y* is a very common way of making an evaluation in spoken language. Likewise, *Why don't you … ?* is a common way of framing a suggestion.

  The way that specific **speech acts** (also called **functions**), such as complementing, suggesting, requesting, offering, and so on, are typically realized comprises part of a speaker's **pragmatic knowledge**. Pragmatic knowledge is knowing how to do things with language, taking into account its contexts of use. This, in turn, means knowing how to perform and interpret specific speech acts. Knowing that one way of framing a request is *Would you mind if … ,* as in *Would you mind if I turn the volume down?,* is part of pragmatic knowledge. It is also knowing that speech acts can be realized indirectly – that, for example, the statement *the music is very loud* has the force of a request (to turn the music down), if uttered in certain contexts.

  Because speech acts often have an instrumental function, in that they involve getting people to do things, they typically form one part of a reciprocal exchange. For example, it is normal to respond to a request with some kind of agreement:

  > Would you mind if I turn the volume down?
  > Not at all.

  Paired utterances like this, in which the second is dependent on the first, are called **adjacency pairs**. Questions and answers are the most common form of adjacency pair, as in:

| Simon: | Have you ever eaten kedgeree since? |
| Kath: | Oh yes I love kedgeree. |

But also greetings, requests, invitations and offers, compliments, reprimands, and apologies are all exchanges that are typically realized by means of adjacency pairs. Often, too, they are quite formulaic, as in the case of greetings:

How do you do?
How do you do?

In fact, many so-called pairs have a three-part structure, where the first speaker adds some kind of evaluation:

Would you mind if I turn the volume down?
Not at all.
*Thanks.*

Three-part exchanges are very common in classroom talk:

| Teacher: | What's the past of the verb *to go*? |
| Student: | *Went.* |
| Teacher: | Good. |

This three-part instructional sequence is called an **IRF exchange**, IRF standing for **initiate – respond – follow-up**.

Longer sequences of paired utterances are also a feature of the *openings* and *closings* of conversations. Take, for example, this closing of a telephone conversation:

| Well, I'd better get back to work. | *pre-closing* |
| Hmm, me too. | |
| So, I'll speak to you later. | |
| OK, then. | |
| Have a good day. | *closing* |
| You, too. | |
| Bye. | |
| Bye bye. | |

Speech act knowledge, then, means knowing not just how particular speech acts are typically realized, but how such speech acts fit into the longer exchanges that form units of talk.

- **The co-operative principle**
  Interpreting the communicative force of speech acts, and knowing how to respond appropriately, assumes that participants in a speech event are 'playing the game according to the same rules'. For example, if you ask a question, you assume that what your interlocutor says in response is an answer. Or, if not, that it is nevertheless relevant to what you have just

asked. For example, in this exchange, Bea's response to Andy's question is also a question:

| Andy: | What does *pragmatics* mean? |
| Bea: | Do you have an hour or two? |

Because Andy takes for granted that Bea is co-operating in the conversation, he has to assume that she isn't ignoring his question and initiating another conversational topic altogether, but that her question is somehow relevant to his question. So he says:

| Andy: | Complicated, huh? Just give me the short answer. |

Andy correctly understood that Bea's answer implied that pragmatics is a complicated subject, not amenable to a snappy definition. The assumption that, in the absence of any evidence to the contrary, speakers are co-operating with one another forms what is called the **co-operative principle**, which the philosopher Grice elaborated into four maxims:

1 Quantity: Make your contribution just as informative as required.
2 Quality: Make your contribution one that is true.
3 Relation: Make your contribution relevant.
4 Manner: Avoid obscurity and ambiguity. Be brief and orderly.

Sometimes it is not easy to abide by these maxims, and speakers will often indicate that they may be at risk of violating one of them. For example, in this continuation to Andy and Bea's conversation, Bea starts by saying:

> Well, *at the risk of oversimplifying matters*, pragmatics is about language in context ...

She is aware that her answer may be less informative than necessary, thereby running counter to the maxim of quantity. On the other hand, she might have said:

> Well, *I may be wrong but I think* pragmatics is about language in context ...

which would indicate that she is aware that her answer may not be accurate, hence a potential violation of the maxim of quality. The frequency of such hedges is a good indication of the extent to which speakers are aware of the rules underlying the joint construction of meaningful talk.

• **Politeness**
The rules of conversational co-operation should not be confused with **politeness**. In fact, given the choice between saying the truth and not hurting someone's feelings, speakers will usually opt for the latter, as in this instance:

| Bea: | What did you think of my presentation? |
| Andy: | I thought it was very well researched. |

Because the research is only one aspect of the presentation, Andy is not really making his contribution as informative as required (thus he is flouting the maxim of quantity). He does this in order not to threaten Bea's **face**, that is, her social standing and sense of self-worth. Contrast his 'faint praise' with a more direct affront to face, such as *I didn't like it very much*. Politeness, then, refers to the way we take other speakers' face needs into account.

Languages employ an elaborate armoury of means to avoid threats to face. The use of politeness markers, such as *please* and *thank you* (or their equivalents), are universal. In some languages, positive politeness is encoded in the pronoun system. In French, for example, speakers can choose between *tu* and *vous*, according to the degree of familiarity or respect they wish to convey. In English, as in many languages, the use of distancing devices, such as past tense forms and modal verbs, helps soften the potential threat to face of requests or commands:

> *I was wondering* if you were free on Friday.
> *Could* you turn the lights out when you leave?

Knowledge of how politeness is encoded in the language is obviously a crucial component of knowing how to speak.

- **Register**

Politeness requires of speakers a sensitivity to context, especially the **tenor** of the context – that is, the relationship between speakers, including such factors as relative status and familiarity. Other factors in the context of the speech event will also impact on the language used, particularly on its degree of formality. (Note that formality and politeness intersect, but that they are not the same thing: you can be formal and rude, just as you can be informal and polite.)

Along with tenor, the linguist Michael Halliday identified two other key dimensions of context: the **field** and the **mode**. The field of a speech event refers to the *what* of the event – what is going on, what is being talked about, such as 'a lecture on nutrition', or 'a conversation about food'. The tenor, as we have seen, refers to the *who*, and the mode refers to the *how* – the choice of channel, such as whether the speech event is conducted over the phone as opposed to face-to-face, or in real-time as opposed to prerecorded. Together, these three contextual factors – field, tenor, and mode – influence the speaker's choice of **register**, such as where the speech event lies on a continuum from formal to informal, and whether it is characterized by jargon and other in-group language forms. The register of a university lecture on the topic of nutrition will differ markedly from a conversation between friends on the subject of domestic science. You wouldn't expect to hear the university lecturer say: *Kedgeree, I remember saying to my mum, I've got to take a pound of fish next week we're making kedgeree … .* In fact, even the term *mum* would sound out of place.

A speaker's knowledge, then, involves knowing what language choices are appropriate, given the register variables of field, tenor, and mode.

### Grammar

It is theoretically possible to have short conversations where each utterance consists of nothing but a single word or short phrase, as in this invented example:

| | |
|---|---|
| **A:** | Coffee? |
| **B:** | Thanks. |
| **A:** | Milk? |
| **B:** | Please. |
| **A:** | Sugar? |
| **B:** | No, thanks. |

In this instance, context factors, including the lack of formality, make the use of complex language unnecessary. But to sustain a conversation like this over a variety of topics with a number of speakers would be virtually impossible. The effect would be like baby talk. In order to generate a much more sophisticated range of meanings, the resources of the language's grammar need to be enlisted.

This does not mean, however, that the grammar of speech is identical to the grammar of written texts. We have already noted how the demands of producing speech in real-time with minimal planning opportunities places considerable constraints on the kind of complexity speakers can achieve. A sentence like that last one is much more typical of written language than of spontaneous spoken language. Spoken, it might have sounded like this:

> Speaking, you're doing it in real-time, you don't have much planning time, so it tends to be less complex than ... or rather it's a different kind of complexity, than, say, writing.

Another distinguishing feature of spoken grammar is the three-part division of utterances into a body plus optional head and tail slots, as in:

| head | body | tail |
|---|---|---|
| Kedgeree | I remember saying to my mum ... | |
| | This is really nice | this Rioja |

Not to be confused with tails are **tags**, typically question tags, with which the speaker makes a direct appeal for the listener's agreement, consent, and so on. They therefore have a primarily interpersonal function. For example:

| body | tail | tag |
|---|---|---|
| This is really nice | this Rioja | isn't it? |

Question tags are virtually non-existent in written language, apart from in fiction, but they are extremely common in speaking, comprising a quarter of all questions. Other ways of forming a tag include expressions like *right? no? ok?* and the vernacular *innit?*

Other features of spoken grammar that are less rules than tendencies are a preference for direct speech rather than reported speech, as in:

> she said 'you don't want to be making kedgeree' and she said 'we don't like it'

and the use of **vague language**, as in:

> It's a sort of old colonial dish

Vagueness expressions are used not only to fill pauses, but also to reduce the assertiveness of statements. This is a way of fulfilling Grice's 'maxim of quality' (*make your contribution one that is true*). It is also a way of reducing the face-threatening potential of an assertion – of being less 'bold'. Writing, however, typically requires greater precision, or may use other means, such as modality, to reduce the assertiveness of statements (as in this sentence).

We have also seen how spoken language tolerates **ellipsis**, as in *Might be great*, where in writing *It might be great* would normally be preferred.

Finally, there are a number of features of spoken grammar that are the audible effects of real-time processing difficulties – what we will call **performance effects**. These include the use of hesitations (*erm, uh*), repeats, false starts, incomplete utterances, and **syntactic blends**, i.e. utterances that 'blend' two grammatical structures, as in *I've been to China … in 1998*.

Features of spoken grammar that distinguish it from written grammar are summarized in this table:

| Written grammar | Spoken grammar |
|---|---|
| Sentence is the basic unit of construction | Clause is the basic unit of construction |
| Clauses are often embedded (subordination) | Clauses are usually added (co-ordination) |
| Subject + verb + object construction | Head + body + tail construction |
| Reported speech favoured | Direct speech favoured |
| Precision favoured | Vagueness tolerated |
| Little ellipsis | A lot of ellipsis |
| No question tags | Many question tags |
| No performance effects | Performance effects, including:<br>• hesitations<br>• repeats<br>• false starts<br>• incompletion<br>• syntactic blends |

Other differences between written and spoken grammar have to do with the distribution of particular items. We noted, for example, that personal pronouns and determiners (such as *I, you, my, our* ...) are more frequent in spoken language than they are in written. The following list summarizes facts about the distribution and frequency of verb forms in spoken language:

- present tense forms outnumber past tense forms by 2:1.
- simple forms outnumber progressive and perfect forms by over 10:1.
- the past perfect and present perfect continuous are rare.
- passive verbs account for only 2% of all finite verb forms in speech.
- *will*, *would*, and *can* are extremely common in speech.

### Vocabulary

The Russian theorist Bakhtin hypothesized a 'fully meaningful and complete' conversation between two people in a room that consisted of nothing but the one word: *Well!* In fact, a lot of conversation does consist to a very large extent of such common words and short phrases as *well*, *yeah*, *but*, *I know* etc. Researchers, using large databases (**corpora**) of transcribed speech, have demonstrated that the fifty most frequent words in spoken English make up nearly 50% of all talk. (This contrasts with a figure of less than 40% of coverage for the fifty most frequent words in written English.) As an example, the word *well* occurs about nine times more often in speech than in writing.

*Well* is an example of a discourse marker (see above) which is very common in spoken interaction. Spoken language also has a relatively high proportion of words and expressions that express the speaker's attitude (**stance**) to what is being said. These include ways of expressing doubt and certainty, such as *probably* and *maybe*, as well as ways of emphasizing the factual nature of what is being said, such as *really* and *actually*.

Speakers also employ a lot of words and expressions that express positive or negative **appraisal**. This is due to the fact that a lot of speech has an interpersonal function, and, by identifying what it is they like or don't like, speakers are able to express solidarity with one another. In this short extract from the kedgeree conversation, the appraisal language is underlined:

| (52) | Kath: | It's one of those <u>ridiculously</u> old-fashioned dishes that they make you cook in domestic science = |
| (53) | Hilda: | This is <u>really nice</u> this Rioja |
| (54) | Nick: | Well why don't you try making some? Might be <u>great</u> |

Finally, we have already mentioned the prominent use of **deictic** language in speech – that is, words and expressions that 'point' to the place, time, and participants in the immediate or a more distant context. The exact referents of deictic expressions – that is, the exact things or people they refer to – are only recoverable by reference to the context. Here are some common deictic expressions:

| spatial deixis | temporal deixis | person deixis |
|---|---|---|
| here, this (place, thing etc) | now, this (time) | I, me |
| there, that (place, thing etc) | then, that (time) | you, your |

So far we have talked about the types of words that are common in speech, but we haven't said anything about the number. How many words do speakers know? Here we need to distinguish between the [...] (their **productive** vocabulary) and the words that [...] **receptive** vocabulary). Research suggests that the for[...] size of the latter. And the number of words used in speaki[...] number used in writing. That is to say, in speech fewer wo[...] According to some estimates, a vocabulary of just 2,500 words c[...] 95% of spoken text (compared to 80% of written text).

- **Chunks**

  As we saw in the discussion of Kath's kedgeree story in Chapter [...] speakers achieve fluency through the use of prefabricated chunks. These are sequences of speech that are not assembled word by word but have been pre-assembled through repeated use and are now retrievable as single units. Chunks can be defined very broadly as any combination of words which occur together with more than random frequency. They are also known as **lexical phrases**, **holophrases**, **formulaic language**, and '**prefabs**'. Of the different types of chunk, the following are the most common:

  - **collocations** – such as *densely populated, rich and famous, set the table*
  - **phrasal verbs** – such as *get up, log on, run out of, go on about*
  - **idioms, catchphrases** and **sayings** – such as *part and parcel, make ends meet, as cool as a cucumber, speak of the devil*
  - **sentence frames**, i.e. the fixed components of sentences, especially at the beginnings of sentences, that 'frame' open slots – such as *would you like a ... ? the thing is ... , what really gets me is ...*
  - **social formulas** – such as *see you later, have a nice day, mind your head*
  - **discourse markers** – such as *if you ask me, by the way, I take your point, to cut a long story short ...*

In the following short conversational extract between two Australian speakers of English, the likely chunks have been underlined (likely, because, without a more extensive study of each speaker's language, it is not easy to determine what is prefabricated as opposed to what is a novel construction):

| | |
|---|---|
| <S 02> | They were awake at five-thirty Stefan. |
| <S 01> | Yeah. |
| <S 02> | It's way too early after a night like they had last night. |
| <S 01> | Yeah that's right. ... Yeah. You live and learn. |
| <S 02> | And sometimes you don't live and learn. Sometimes you live and repeat and repeat and repeat. |
| <S 01> | [chuckles] Would you like a cup of tea? |
| <S 02> | No thanks. I'm sick of that alarm going off all the time. |
| <S 01> | Yeah. |
| <S 02> | Don't you? |
| <S 01> | Yeah. What can you do? |

Even from this short extract, it's clear that chunks make up a large proportion of spoken language.

s estimate that a native speaker may have hundreds
...iese chunks to draw on, and that this accounts for
...re saw with the race-caller on page 7) but also for
...liomaticity is meant the fact that, out of all the many
...cally acceptable ways of expressing an idea, speakers
...inity tend to conform to what other speakers do. For
...perfect sense, and it is grammatically correct, to say *it's
...'s forty past five*, or *it's two thirds past five*, yet the 'done'
...this idea is *it's twenty to six*.

...wledge that a proficient speaker has access to, then,
...a few thousand words, but of a much greater number of
...corpora are starting to provide information as to which
...the most frequently used. For example, in a recent study
...en US English idioms, one researcher listed the following
as some of the most frequent: *kind of, sort of, of course, in terms of, in fact, deal
with, at all, as well, make sure, go through, first of all, in other words.*

## Phonology

The 'lowest level' of knowledge a speaker draws on is that of pronunciation.
Normally, the way we pronounce individual words, and the sounds that they
are composed of, is not something that involves conscious choices. Words are
stored along with their pronunciation and do not need to be reconstituted
from scratch each time they are used. Occasionally, however, speakers will
adjust their pronunciation to take account of the social context, so as not
to sound too 'posh', for example. Or they will adopt an accent or a quality
of voice for a particular dramatic effect. When, for example, Kath told her
kedgeree story, she adopted – and exaggerated – her mother's accent, to the
amusement of her friends.

One area of pronunciation, however, where significant choices are
available to speakers is in **intonation**. Intonation serves both to separate
the stream of speech into blocks of information (called **tone units**) and to
mark information within these units as being significant. In English, there
is a fundamental association between high pitch and new information. So,
within each tone unit, information that is being added to the discourse is
made prominent through the use of a step up in pitch. Intonation also serves
to signal the connections between tone units. Typically, a rise in pitch at the
end of the tone unit (that is, after the last stressed word) implies some kind
of continuation; a fall in pitch suggests completion.

In the following extract from Kath's story, the three functions of intonation
(segmentation, prominence, and cohesion) are shown working in unison.
The tone units are marked with vertical lines, and the words (or the parts
of them) that are given prominence through a rise in pitch are capitalized.
Pitch changes at the boundaries of tone units are marked by rising or falling
arrows:

KEDgeree ↗ | I reMEMber saying to my MUM ↗ | I've got to take a POUND
of FISH next week ↗ | we're making KEDgeree ↘ | and SHE said ↗ | you don't
want to be making KEDgeree ↗ | and she SAID ↗ | we don't LIKE it ↘ |

words that speakers use
they recognize (their
...er is only half the
...g is less than the
...ds go further.
...vers nearly

24

A further point to note here is the use of a marked rise in pitch on the first word of the story (*Kedgeree*), separating it from the preceding and surrounding discourse. This use of intonation to mark the beginning of a new stage in the discourse – equivalent to starting a new paragraph in writing – is called a **paratone**. It is very perceptible when news readers, for example, move from one story to the next, and it is balanced by an equally marked drop in pitch at the end of each story. Likewise, Kath's closing comment on her anecdote ends on a 'dying fall':

> it was so inappropriate for the first year comprehensive school kids to be making ↘

And, if you were reading this paragraph aloud, you would also no doubt finish on a falling paratone.

**Speech conditions**

Kath was able to tell her story fluently because she knew it, she had told it before, and she was among friends. This suggests that the conditions in which speaking occurs play a crucial role in determining the degree of fluency that is achievable. What are these conditions? That is, what factors make speaking easy or difficult? Researchers have isolated a number of factors, of which the following seem to be the most important. They have been divided into three categories: **cognitive** factors, **affective** (that is, emotional) factors, and **performance** factors.

### Cognitive factors

- *Familiarity with the topic:* the greater the familiarity, the easier the speaking task; this is why it is generally easier to talk about your job, or your family, than it is to talk about something very removed from your day-to-day life.
- *Familiarity with the genre:* giving a lecture or a speech will be harder if you're unfamiliar with those particular genres.
- *Familiarity with the interlocutors:* generally speaking, the better you know the people you are talking to and the more shared knowledge you can assume, the easier it will be.
- *Processing demands:* if the speech event involves complex mental processing, such as that involved in describing a complicated procedure without recourse to illustrations, it will be more difficult than if not.

### Affective factors

- *Feelings towards the topic and/or the participants:* generally, if you are well disposed to the topic you are talking about, and/or to the other participants, the easier it is likely to be.
- *Self-consciousness:* being 'put on the spot' can cause anxiety which will have a negative effect on performance; likewise, knowing (or believing) that you are being evaluated can be prejudicial.

### Performance factors

- *Mode:* speaking face-to-face, where you can closely monitor your interlocutor's responses and where you can use gesture and eye-contact, is generally easier than speaking over the telephone, for example.

- *Degree of collaboration:* giving a presentation on your own is generally harder than doing it with colleagues because in the former case you can't count on peer support.
- *Discourse control:* on the other hand, it is often easier if you can control the direction of events, rather than being subject to someone else's control.
- *Planning and rehearsal time:* generally, the more time to prepare, the easier the task will be; telling a joke is usually easier the second time round.
- *Time pressure:* if there is a degree of urgency, it is likely to increase the difficulty for the speaker.
- *Environmental conditions:* trying to speak against a background of loud music or in poor acoustic conditions (as in many classrooms!) is difficult.

The above factors do not necessarily predict the difficulty or ease of speaking since they also interact with personality factors, such as introversion and extroversion. It is not always the case, for example, that being put on the spot, or urgency, can have negative effects: some speakers respond positively to such pressure. Likewise, physiological factors such as tiredness can undermine performance. Nevertheless, the above factors offer a useful template for predicting the degree of fluency speakers are likely to achieve. (And, as we shall see in Chapter 6, they provide criteria for the selecting and adapting of classroom speaking tasks.)

**Conclusions**

We started this chapter by making a distinction between what speakers *can do* – that is the mental and physiological processes involved in speaking – and what speakers *know* – that is the knowledge base that speakers draw on that enables these processes.

The kinds of knowledge that speakers bring to the skill of speaking comprise extralinguistic knowledge, such as background knowledge of topic and culture, and linguistic knowledge, including discourse knowledge, speech act knowledge, and knowledge of grammar, vocabulary, and phonology.

**Looking ahead**

So far we have described speaking skills and speaker knowledge insofar as they relate to highly-skilled, knowledgeable speakers, making no distinction between speaking in a first or a second (or third, or fourth etc) language. But speakers of another language do not, initially, have easy access to these skills and this knowledge. In the next chapter, we will look at the implications of this skills and knowledge gap, and discuss general approaches to how it might be bridged.

# 3 Speaking in another language

*I have crossed an ocean*
*I have lost my tongue*
*from the root of the old one*
*a new one has sprung*
Grace Nichols

- **Differences between L1 and L2 speaking**

- **Communication strategies**

- **What L2 speakers need to know**

- **Availability for use: implications for teaching**

## Differences between L1 and L2 speaking

The description, offered in the preceding chapters, of how spoken fluency is achieved, has made no distinction between the speaking of a first language (L1) and the speaking of another language (L2). We have discussed the skills and kinds of knowledge involved in achieving fluency as if these were absolute qualities that all speakers share. Clearly this is not the case. Even among L1 speakers there can be wide variations in the degree of fluency that individuals demonstrate. These differences are exacerbated when it comes to speaking in a language different from your own. The inevitable lack of fluency involved is a source of frustration and even embarrassment, as attested by these quotes from learners of English, in response to the question: *Which aspects of your English do you most want to improve?*

'My weak points in English is speaking and listening. I suppose I am not so bad at reading and writing, but especially, my speaking is awful. I want to improve my speaking ability as once I had.'

'I would like to improve my spoken English and my pronunciation. I think I have terrible Russian accent. Therefore I'm very shy to speak.'

'This is the problem, I have been learning English long, but I can't speak, I understand the conversation but I can't answer immediately as I like.'

'The problem is to speak English with other people face to face. I can't find words. I always use the same sentences.'

'I know I need to practice my speaking a lot. During all my life, I have been doing grammar and reading, but nobody has taught me how to speak English. I think that this skill is always forgotten when someone teaches English.'

'Sometimes I use English in my work and this is always a painful moment for me in which my heart is in my boots and I despairing search the words.'

These quotes identify some key factors that can contribute to a lack of L2 fluency, and in particular how a lack of automaticity can inhibit face-to-face interaction, quite independently of how much grammatical and lexical knowledge a speaker has. Shortage of opportunities for **practice** is identified as an important contributing factor to speaking failure. And by practice is meant, not practice of grammar and vocabulary, but practice of interactive speaking itself. The combined effect of these deficiencies is a lack of confidence and often an acute sense of anxiety when it comes to speaking ('my heart is in my boots').

What can be done about this? The comment that 'this skill [i.e. speaking] is always forgotten when someone teaches English' is astute. All language teaching methods (apart from the most bookish) prioritize speaking, but less as a skill in its own right than as a means of practising grammar. Even in relatively communication-oriented methodologies, speaking activities are often simply ways of rehearsing pre-selected grammar items or functional expressions. If speaking-as-skill is dealt with, it is often dealt with only at the level of pronunciation. Frequently, training and practice in the skill of interactive real-time talk, with all its attendant discourse features, is relegated to the chat stage at the beginning and end of lessons. It is this lack of genuine speaking opportunities which accounts for many students' feeling that, however much grammar and vocabulary they know, they are insufficiently prepared for speaking in the world beyond the classroom.

How then does L2 speaking differ from L1 speaking? In terms of the stages of mental processing involved, there is probably not much difference at all. Like L1 speakers, L2 speakers also produce speech through a process of conceptualizing, then formulating, and finally articulating, during which time they are also self-monitoring. At the same time, they will be attending to their interlocutors, adjusting their message accordingly, and negotiating the management of conversational turns. The skills of speaking, therefore, are essentially the same and should, in theory, be transferable from the speaker's first language into the second.

What is significantly different is, of course, the language itself. L2 speakers' knowledge of the L2, including its vocabulary and grammar, is rarely as extensive or as established as their knowledge of their L1. They are like the student who said, 'I can't find words. I always use·the same sentences'.

On the other hand, the problem may be less a lack of knowledge than the unavailability of that knowledge. It has not become sufficiently integrated into their existing language knowledge, or it has been so seldom accessed, that it is not yet easily retrievable. The process of arranging the grammar or retrieving the word is not yet automatic. They then feel like the student who 'despairing search[es for] the words'.

The process may be complicated by a tendency to formulate the utterance first in the L1 and then 'translate' it into the L2, with an obvious cost in terms of speed. Furthermore, pressure to be accurate – to avoid making humiliating errors – may mean that the self-monitoring process is overused and over-prolonged, again with a negative effect in terms of fluency. These extended mental deliberations that speakers can enter into are well captured in this description of his students by Humphrey McQueen, a visiting Australian professor of economics in Japan:

> Talking with them has been a trial of patience as I watch their faces work like computer screens. Inside, their brains are composing sentences, searching for the most appropriate word, then running the draft past their mind's eye for grammatical mistakes. Finally, the sentence is allowed out. I reply. They look uncertain, sometimes ask for a re-run, before their facial screen goes blank while a new sentence is under construction. They seem terrified of making a mistake, which is no way to become fluent. Yet their knowledge of formal grammar is far greater than Australian undergraduates and they have extensive vocabularies.

In more scientific terms, these students are having trouble distributing their attentional capacity between planning and articulation, not to mention the added demand of coping with new input. Also, their anxiety is causing excessive self-monitoring: they are what the researcher Stephen Krashen termed **monitor overusers**.

Of course, not all L2 speakers agonize to this extent. In fact, some speakers adopt a completely different strategy, preferring to use (and possibly overuse) the little language they have at their linguistic 'fingertips', so to speak, rather than construct novel utterances from scratch. Not all Japanese learners are as portrayed above; Pico Iyer describes another Japanese speaker who has achieved communicative fluency using minimal means:

> Sachiko-san was as unabashed and unruly in her embrace of English as most of her compatriots were reticent and shy. … She was happy to plunge ahead without a second thought for grammar, scattering meanings and ambiguities as she went. Plurals were made singular, articles were dropped, verbs were rarely inflected, and word order was exploded – often, in fact, she seemed to be making Japanese sentences with a few English words thrown in. Often, moreover, to vex the misunderstandings further, she spoke both languages at once … .

Rather than 'computing' each utterance using the relatively slow, albeit more accurate, rule-based system, Sachiko-san seems to be drawing on a store of memorized words and chunks. And even when Sachiko's memory fails, all is not lost: she simply resorts to Japanese. She knows how to make the best use of all available resources and has at her command a variety of different strategies to get her message across, even if this means resorting to what sounds like baby-talk. The successful use of such strategies in order to communicate in a second language is called **strategic competence**.

**Communication strategies**

Strategic competence is achieved by means of what are called **communication strategies**. Some commonly encountered communication strategies are:

- circumlocution: such as *I get a red in my head* to mean *shy*
- word coinage: such as *vegetarianist* for *vegetarian*
- foreignizing a word: such as turning the Spanish word *una carpeta* (meaning a file for papers) into the English-sounding *a carpet*

- approximation: using an alternative, related word, such as using *work table* for *workbench*
- using an all-purpose word, such as *stuff, thing, make, do*
- language switch: using the L1 word or expression (also called **code-switching**)
- paralinguistics: using gesture, mime, and so on, to convey the intended meaning
- appealing for help, e.g. by leaving an utterance incomplete, as in:

> Speaker 1: The taxi driver get angry, he lose his, erm, how you say?
> Speaker 2: temper
> Speaker 1: he lose his temper and he shout me

Of course, the speaker might decide that the message is simply not achievable, by whatever means, and adopt what is called an **avoidance strategy**, such as abandoning the message altogether or replacing the original message with one that is less ambitious.

Another type of strategy, called a **discourse strategy**, is the wholesale borrowing by the speaker of segments of other speakers' utterances, often in the form of unanalysed units, as in this instance:

> Speaker 1: When did you last see your brother?
> Speaker 2: Last see your brother six years ago …

A related discourse strategy is the repetition of one's own previous utterance:

> Speaker 1: The woman hear a noise …
> Speaker 2: What kind of noise?
> Speaker 1: The woman hear a noise, loud one …

Such strategies are similar to the production strategies used by proficient speakers (see page 7), in that they help 'buy' valuable processing time and thus maintain the illusion of fluency.

It should be obvious that a repertoire of communication and discourse strategies can prove very useful for learners in that it allows them to achieve a degree of communicative effectiveness beyond their immediate linguistic means. However, researchers are in two minds about the long-term benefits of such strategies. While they may provide learners with an initial conversational 'foothold', they may also lead to the premature closing down of the learner's developing language system (or **interlanguage**) – a process that is sometimes called **fossilization**. Certain learners seem to become dependent on their strategic competence at the expense of their overall linguistic competence. Sachiko – in the example quoted above – succeeds at being highly communicative, but at what future cost? There appears to be a trade-off between early fluency and later interlanguage development.

Sachiko's English was probably a product of the conditions in which she used it. It had developed in face-to-face encounters, with little time for careful planning or self-monitoring. Nor, perhaps, did she possess the kind of learned grammar knowledge necessary in order to fine-tune her utterances, even if time had been available to do so. She had no choice, therefore, but to depend on words, including the liberal use of ready-made chunks, rather than on grammar.

As we saw in Chapter 2, the conditions in which speech occurs exert a powerful influence on its quality, in terms of its fluency, its accuracy, and its complexity. So, depending on the kinds of conditions their speaking is subject to, learners are likely to adopt different coping strategies. Some, like Sachiko, who are using their L2 in real-life encounters, with little or no chance for careful planning or monitoring, may opt for relying on words rather than grammar to get their meaning across. This, however, may have harmful effects on their long-term interlanguage development. Others, with more time on their hands, will settle for a more analytic, grammar-based approach, but they will pay the price in fluency.

Ideally, of course, learners will find a balance between speed and planning, between fast access and slow analysis. And, in the end, the kind of speaking they achieve should be the one that is most suited to their individual needs. Where accuracy is less a priority, as in Sachiko's case, a non-analytic strategy may work best. On the other hand, where the long-term goals of the learner involve speaking with precision, a jump-start into fluency may be counterproductive.

However, a lifetime spent studying grammar is no guarantee that speaking will come naturally, either. As the student (on page 27) complained 'During all my life, I have been doing grammar and reading, but nobody has taught me how to speak English'. Knowledge that is not 'available for use' is knowledge that is dead on the page.

And this raises two fundamental questions facing teachers of speaking:

- What knowledge is required for speaking?
- How can this knowledge be made available for use?

We'll consider each of these questions in turn.

**What L2 speakers need to know**

In the previous chapter, we reviewed and listed the kinds of knowledge that proficient speakers draw on when speaking. Let's revisit that list, and evaluate how the linguistic aspects of speaker knowledge apply to second language speaking. (By definition, extralinguistic knowledge, such as knowledge of topic, context, and familiarity with the other speakers need not concern us, since this will be either present or absent irrespective of the language spoken.)

### Sociocultural knowledge

The value of teaching sociocultural knowledge, i.e. the culturally embedded rules of social behaviour, is debatable. Many of these so-called rules are based on flimsy, often hearsay, evidence. And they can tend to reinforce stereotypes, to the point of caricature. The notion that all British speakers of English talk mainly about the weather, do not suffer conversational silences, and say *sorry* all the time, is about as well-founded as the idea that they also wear bowler hats and carry furled umbrellas.

Moreover, for many learners nowadays such 'rules' may be irrelevant since they will be learning English as an International Language (EIL) rather than the English that is used in, say, Birmingham or Baltimore. What is more important than learning local sociocultural customs might be to develop **intercultural competence** – that is, the ability to manage cross-cultural encounters irrespective of the culture of the language being used, and taking into account that difference and ambiguity are inherent in *all* communication. Simply knowing how to ask *How do you do that here?* may be more useful than a list of 'dos and don'ts'.

### Genre knowledge

Genre knowledge includes knowing how different speech events are structured, and this will be particularly relevant to learners whose specific purposes for learning English include mastering spoken genres of a more formal type, such as giving business presentations or academic lectures. For more day-to-day communication, such as service encounters or casual conversation, the genres are likely to be either easily transferable from the learner's L1 or so loosely defined as to be difficult to teach in any formal sense anyway.

This does not mean that genres should be ignored or that features of language should be introduced out of their generic context. On the contrary, because genres are recognizable across cultures, they serve as a useful way of providing learners with new language in a familiar frame. The question *Anything else?* will make more sense when it is embedded in a shopping dialogue than if it were presented in isolation. What learners probably do not need, though, is to be taught the generic structure itself. Teaching a learner that you greet shopkeepers on entering a store, and then wait to be asked what you want, may be somewhat condescending. Likewise, teaching learners that speakers take turns in conversation is tantamount to teaching L2 readers that books have pages. What the learners need, more than the generic structure of the interaction, are specific ways of realizing particular interactional moves. In other words, they need speech-act knowledge.

### Speech acts

Just as learners need to know how specific discourse moves are realized, they also need to know the ways specific speech acts (also called **functions**) are typically encoded. For example, the following ways of offering advice or suggestions are common:

| | |
|---|---|
| I'd ... (if I were you) | You ought to ... |
| You'd better ... | Why don't you ... ? |
| If you want my advice, you ... | |

On the other hand, the following ways are less common in informal spoken English:

I advise you to ...
My advice to you would be ...
What I suggest is ...
I have a suggestion ...

While these, all perfectly possible from a grammatical point of view, never or rarely occur:

> Why do you not ... ?
> I have some advice ...
> My suggestion to you would be ...
> If you want my suggestion, ...

This suggests that learners cannot necessarily intuit the way that speech acts are customarily realized, nor the way that they are realized in spoken, as opposed to written, English. There is a good case, therefore, for the explicit teaching of these forms. Apart from anything, they are typically realized in short, memorable formulas, and therefore can be learned and stored as extended lexical items, much in the way that generations of tourists have used phrasebooks to get by with.

### Register

Learners will also need to know how to adapt these speech-act formulas for different situations, according to such context variables as the status of the person they are talking to. Exposure to different registers of speech, plus directed attention to the ways in which spoken language is made more or less formal, should be sufficient, at least for general English purposes, to sensitize learners to this area. Role-plays (see page 96) are probably one of the best ways of practising different constellations of register variables, such as the differences that social status makes.

### Discourse

Discourse knowledge, as noted in the last chapter, involves using grammar and vocabulary in order to connect speaking turns and to signal speaker intentions. Discourse knowledge also assumes an understanding of how speaking turns are managed – knowing that, for example, talk is collaboratively constructed through the taking and yielding of turns. However, since this is a universal feature of spoken interaction, it is not something learners need to be taught. They simply need to know how these turn-management moves are realized in the second language, through the use, primarily, of discourse markers. The list of discourse markers in Chapter 1 (page 9) would serve as a useful starting point in this area.

### Grammar

We noted in the preceding chapters that grammar knowledge for speaking purposes consists largely of those grammar systems that favour rapid, real-time speech production. Since spontaneous speech is produced in clause-length units rather than sentence-length ones, a sentence grammar will be of limited usefulness for speaking. It is sentence grammar, however, that has always been the main focus of language teaching. Learners are taught to manipulate relatively lengthy and complex constructions that are more typical of written than of spoken language. To take one example: the conditional *would* is traditionally first taught as an element of the second

*I would never eat*

and third conditional constructions, which consist of an *if*-clause and a *would*-clause (*if I had the time, I would study harder; if I'd had the time, I would have studied harder*), rather than being taught as an element of *would*-clauses on their own (*I would never eat horse meat*). But analyses of corpora of spoken English show that *would*-clauses occur four times more often without an associated *if*-clause than with one.

Likewise, learners are taught grammar items without a clear distinction being made between spoken and written grammar. Of course, there is a great deal of overlap, but there are certain structures that are much less frequent in speech than in writing, such as reported speech, subordinate clauses, relative clauses, and the passive. On the other hand, some features of spoken syntax (such as heads and tails, and ellipsis – see page 21), get little or no attention at all in many mainstream ELT courses.

A core grammar for informal speaking would probably need to include the following items:

- a command of present and past simple, and the ability to use the latter to sequence narratives.
- familiarity with the use of the continuous and perfect **aspect** forms of verbs, both to frame and background information in narratives, as in *I was coming out of the supermarket … it'd been raining …* .
- a knowledge of the most frequently occurring **modal** and **semi-modal** verbs (i.e. *can, will, would, have to, going to, used to*).
- the ability to formulate questions, especially *yes/no-* but also *wh*-questions.
- some basic conjunctions (*and, so, but*) in order to string together sequences of clausal and non-clausal units.
- one or two all-purpose quoting expressions, of the *he said … and then I said …* type.

**Vocabulary**

We noted in the last chapter that native speakers employ over 2,500 words to cover 95% of their needs. Learners can probably get by on a lot fewer, maybe half that number, especially for the purposes of casual conversation. Obviously, for more specialized purposes such as business negotiations or academic speaking, they will need more. Short of knowing exactly which words the learners will need, the most useful criterion for selection is probably *frequency*. A working knowledge of the 1,500 most frequent words in English would stand a learner in good stead. Even the top 200 most common words will provide the learner with a lot of conversational mileage, since they include:

- all the common question forming words, such as *where, why, when, how, whose …?*
- all the modal auxiliary verbs: *would, will, can, may, might, should* etc.
- all the pronouns, such as *it, I, me, you, they, us,* and the possessive forms such as *my, your, hers, their*
- the demonstrative pronouns and other common deictic devices (see page 22) such as *this, that, here, there, now, then*

- all the common prepositions, such as *in, on, near, from, after, between*
- the full range of spoken discourse markers (see page 9), such as *well, oh, so, but, and, right, now*
- common backchannel expressions, such as *really, no, what,* and *how* … as in *how awful! how wonderful!*
- common sequencing and linking words, such as *then, first, so, and, or, next*
- common ways of adding emphasis, such as *really, very, just, so*
- common ways of hedging (i.e. reducing assertiveness), such as *actually, quite, rather, sort (of)*
- all-purpose words, such as *thing, things, place, time, way, make* and *do*

Most learners' dictionaries, such as the *Longman Dictionary of Contemporary English* (LDOCE), now highlight high frequency words and even indicate their relative frequency in speech and in writing. Here, for example, is the entry for the verb *bet* in the LDOCE:

**bet**[1] S1 /bet/ *v past tense and past participle* **bet**, *present participle* **betting**

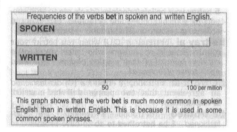

Frequencies of the verbs **bet** in spoken and written English.

This graph shows that the verb **bet** is much more common in spoken English than in written English. This is because it is used in some common spoken phrases.

The formula S1 in the box means that *bet* is in the top 1000 words of spoken English. In fact, *bet* is so common in spoken English that it deserves a special comment:

In the following extract (from data that was used in the preparation of the coursebook *Natural English*), in which a Polish learner is describing a shopping experience, the words that do not fall in the top 2000 words band in spoken English, according to the LDOCE, are underlined. The words that are in the 1000–2000 band are in italics. The words in the 1–1000 band are unmarked.

---

**A:** It happened I think two years ago, I went to a shop. It was <u>Saturday</u>, I usually do my *shopping* on <u>Saturday</u>. So I went to a shop to buy *shoes*, and I went to that particular shop in which I found my *pair* of *shoes* …

**B:** Expensive?

**A:** Yeah, quite expensive.

**B:** How much?

**A:** About <u>forty</u> to <u>fifty</u> pounds, something like that. So I went there, it was full of people and I tried on the shoes that I liked, so I decided to buy them. So I bought them. I went home after that, but it was almost the end of the day, the *shopping* day, so it wasn't left a long time for the shops to close, so when I went home and decided to try on the *shoes* again, I saw that in the bag were two left *shoes*. So I had, well, it was quite an expensive *pair* of *shoes*, so I tried to go back to the shop and *exchange* them so although I knew that they will *exchange* them, I was a bit *worried*. But I was late and the shop was closed already and I had to go on … next day on <u>Sunday</u> to get the proper *pair* of *shoes*.

**B:** Did you manage to get it?

**A:** Yes, *finally*.

---

The learner has told her story using only words within the 2000 top frequency range (apart from four), and the vast majority of the words – 92% of the total words used – are in the top 1000. The student (who was in an advanced class) manages to be communicatively effective using only a limited range of words. (By the way, the fact that *Saturday* and *Sunday*, and *forty* and *fifty*, are relatively infrequent may seem counterintuitive, especially given that these are words that are taught very early in a language course. The fact is that they belong to frequently occurring sets – i.e. days of the week, and numbers – but the frequency of occurrences is distributed across the members within the set. This suggests that there is a case for teaching not just frequent words but frequently occurring *sets* of words.)

The point, made earlier, that *bet* forms part of commonly used phrases, alerts us to the fact that, as important as individual words are, so too are chunks. In the last chapter, we saw how a mental store of memorized chunks is essential if fluency is to be achieved. In fact, knowing that *bet* is very frequent is of little use unless the learner knows that it forms the nucleus of the following high frequency chunks:

> I bet
> I'll bet
> you bet
> wanna bet?
> don't bet on it
> your best bet (is …)
> my bet (is …)
> a safe bet

The problem is that there are a great many more combinations of words than there are individual words. Which chunks are likely to be of use to learners? Until more information about the frequency of chunks becomes available, a rule of thumb might be to focus on the chunks that are associated with the most common words in the language. The frequency of these common words may owe a lot to the fact that they form at least one element of commonly used chunks. It's a safe bet, for example, that the word *bet* is more often used in its idiomatic combinations (*I bet, you bet, wanna bet?*) than it is in its more literal sense, as in *I bet on a horse in the fifth race*.

Moreover, the advantage of learning the formulaic chunks associated with high-frequency words is that many of these form common syntactic strings, such as *be + going + to +* verb as in *it's going to rain*. So, by learning the chunk the learner gets the string – and the grammar – 'for free'.

## Phonology

Finally, we come to phonology, an area which is perhaps the least amenable to conscious control at the moment of articulation. Most adult learners will betray, to varying degrees, the influence of their first language pronunciation when speaking a second language, and this need not be a problem so long as intelligibility is not threatened. Intelligibility, however, is in the ear of the beholder. That is to say, what might be intelligible to one listener is not necessarily intelligible to another.

Native speakers, for example, frequently identify the non-native-like use of stress, rhythm, and intonation as being a greater bar to intelligibility, and a stronger marker of accent, than the way individual vowel and consonant sounds are pronounced. This is particularly acute when lack of fluency segments speech into very short runs, as in this example, where a Japanese speaker is discussing her plan to show pictures of modern Japan to US school children. Stressed words are printed in capital letters, and pause lengths are shown in brackets, in seconds:

> … not only WORDS ↗ (.4) I can SHOW ↗ (.4) the (.4) PICTURES ↗ (.6) HELPED ↗ (.8) STUDENTS ↗ to un- HELP- (.5) STUDENTS ↗ (.2) UNDERSTAND the (.4) JAPANESE CULTURE ↘

As Ann Wennerstrom comments, by speaking in such short bursts, with each word given almost equal emphasis, 'the effect is to obscure the main point of the discourse because every word seems to be singled out as worthy of comment'.

Of course, native speaker judgments are irrelevant if speakers are speaking English as an International Language. The researcher Jennifer Jenkins examined the main causes of communication breakdown when non-native speakers are talking to each other and, on this basis, identified the following areas of pronunciation as being crucial for intelligibility:

- certain 'core' consonant sounds (but not vowels)
- the contrast between long and short vowels (as in *hit* and *heat*)
- consonant clusters, especially those at the beginning of words, such as *pr* in *product*
- sentence stress, i.e. the correct placement of stress in an utterance, especially contrastive stress (*she's my COUSIN, not my sister*)

If this list seems relatively short, it is nevertheless consistent with the view we have taken so far – that fluent spoken English is not simply a function of a wide-ranging knowledge of grammar, an extensive vocabulary, and a native-like pronunciation. In fact, as this chapter has tried to demonstrate, fluency may be achievable with relatively minimal means.

**Availability for use: implications for teaching**

So far we have attempted to answer the first of the two key questions posed on page 31, i.e. what knowledge is required for speaking? Now we can turn to the second question: how can this knowledge be made available for use?

Essentially, to ensure availability for use, there are three processes involved. Learners need to be made aware of features of the target knowledge-base, they need to integrate these features into their existing knowledge-base, and they need to develop the capacity to mobilize these features under real-time conditions. Depending on the view of learning that is adopted, these processes are named, described, and rated differently. There have been at least three theories of language learning that are relevant to the teaching of speaking: **behaviourist**, **cognitivist**, and **sociocultural** theory, and we shall briefly review each in turn.

According to behaviourism, language learning is essentially the formation of good language 'habits' through repeated reinforcement. In its popularized form, **audiolingualism**, the three stages of learning were called **presentation**, **practice**, and **production** (**PPP**). The three-step PPP process was aimed at developing automatic habits largely through classroom processes of modelling, repetition, and controlled practice. PPP was applied originally to the teaching of grammar, but, by extension it has been used to structure the teaching of language skills as well, including speaking. A typical teaching sequence might involve listening to, and imitating, a taped dialogue, followed by repetition of features of the dialogue, and then performance of the dialogue in class.

A cognitivist account of language learning rejects the behaviourist view of the learners as empty vessels waiting to be filled, and instead credits them with an information processing capacity, analogous to computers. According to this view, the learning of a complex skill, like speaking, is seen as a movement from controlled to automatic processing. Initially, conscious attention (or awareness-raising) is applied to the learning of the individual stages (or rules) of a procedure that, through repeated activation, are chunked into a single manageable 'program'. This is integrated into existing knowledge, a stage which will involve some restructuring of the user's linguistic system, and is then readily available for use, with minimal attentional control on the part of the user. This is the stage known as **autonomy**.

In teaching terms, cognitivist theory replaced the PPP model with one that progresses from **awareness-raising**, through **proceduralization**, to **autonomy**. In fact, it is only the first stage that is significantly different, in terms of classroom practice. Awareness-raising implies an *explicit* focus on the rules of the system, whereas strict audiolingual practice insisted on simply imitating models without any explicit attention being given to the rules that generated them.

The cognitivist model prioritizes mental functions over social ones. Sociocultural theory, on the other hand, situates the learning process firmly in its social context. According to this view, all learning – including the learning of a first and a second language – is **mediated** through social and cultural activity. To achieve autonomy in a skill, the learner first needs to experience **other-regulation**, that is, the mediation of a 'better other', whether parent, peer, or teacher. This typically takes the form of **assisted performance**, whereby the teacher interacts with the learner to provide a supportive framework (or **scaffold**) within which the learners can extend their present competence. Through this shared activity, new knowledge is jointly constructed until the learners are in a position to **appropriate** it – i.e. to make it their own – at which stage the scaffolding can be gradually dismantled. Learners are now able to function independently in a state of **self-regulation**. A good example of this is the way an older child will teach a younger one the rules of a game, by both talking and walking it through, until the younger one has got the hang of it.

Learning, according to the sociocultural view, is fundamentally a social phenomenon, requiring both activity and interactivity. In classroom terms, it takes place in cycles of assisted performance, in which learning is collaborative, co-constructed, and scaffolded. For example, learners may set about solving a problem in small groups, during which the teacher intervenes when necessary to provide suggestions or even to model the targeted behaviour.

All three theories have elements in common, especially when these are translated into classroom procedures. The following table attempts to display the relation between different elements of each model:

| behaviourist theory | cognitivist theory | sociocultural theory |
|---|---|---|
| presentation, modelling | awareness-raising | other-regulation |
| practice | proceduralization, restructuring | appropriation |
| production | automaticity, autonomy | self-regulation |

These surface similarities, however, shouldn't be allowed to disguise the fact that each theory reflects a very different conception of the mind. The behaviourist mind is simply a brain, pushed, pulled, and moulded by forces beyond its control. The cognitivist mind is a computerized black box, busily processing input into output. The sociocultural mind is a network, a joint construct of the discourse community through which it is distributed. Each metaphor for the mind clearly has different implications in terms of learning, and of language learning in particular. Nevertheless, each theory incorporates a stage which roughly equates with **awareness**, whereby the learner encounters something new. And each theory attempts to explain how this knowledge is integrated, or **appropriated**, into the learner's existing systems. And finally, each theory accepts that at least some of this new knowledge becomes available for use: it is automated and the learner is **autonomous**.

**Conclusions**

In this chapter we have looked at speaking from the point of view of the learner, coping with the challenge of speaking in a second (or other) language. Essentially, the difficulties that the learner-speaker faces break down into two main areas:

- knowledge factors: the learner doesn't yet know aspects of the language that enable production.
- skills factors: the learner's knowledge is not sufficiently automated to ensure fluency.

As a result, there may also be:

- affective factors, such as lack of confidence or self-consciousness, which might inhibit fluency.

Learners compensate for their insufficient knowledge of the language system by using communication strategies, and they compensate for lack of fluency by using discourse strategies.

Over-reliance on such strategies, however, could lead to premature fossilization of the learner's interlanguage. Fossilization may also result from a preference for a lexical mode of processing, as opposed to a more grammatical one.

In terms of the knowledge base that enables speech, learners need:

- a core grammar.
- a core vocabulary of at least 1000 high-frequency items.
- some common discourse markers.
- a core 'phrasebook' of multi-word units (or chunks).
- formulaic ways of performing common speech acts (such as requesting or inviting).
- mastery of those features of pronunciation that inhibit intelligibility.

Also important is that speakers remember to take into account context factors, including the cultural context and the context of the immediate situation.

In order to activate these knowledge areas and make them available for use in fluent, face-to-face talk, the learning process needs to include at least three stages. Learners need:

- to be made aware of features of the target knowledge-base, i.e. **awareness.**
- to integrate these features into their existing knowledge-base, i.e. **appropriation.**
- to develop the capacity to mobilize these features under real-time conditions and unassisted, i.e. **autonomy**.

**Looking ahead**    In the chapter that follows we will look at the first of these areas – awareness – and suggest ways that learners' awareness of the features of spoken language can be optimized. In the two subsequent chapters, we will consider activities that target appropriation and autonomy.

# 4 Awareness-raising activities

- **Awareness-raising**
- **Using recordings and transcripts**
- **Focusing on selected language features**
- **Using live listening**
- **Using noticing-the-gap activities**

**Awareness-raising**

There are things learners can't easily do, such as retrieving words at speed or achieving long, pause-free runs. This is because they lack certain skills. Subsequent chapters will look more closely at how learners can become more skilful. But there are also things learners don't know, such as what to say in order to signal a change of topic or how to respond appropriately to a difficult request, and this also inhibits their fluency. In these cases, they lack the knowledge. This chapter looks at ways of helping them uncover these gaps in their knowledge.

Activities aimed at helping learners uncover these gaps we will call **awareness activities**, rather than simply **presentation activities**, since the former term allows the possibility of learners discovering – and even filling – their knowledge gaps themselves. The assumption is, though, that the teacher will always be on hand to guide the process and provide support and feedback where necessary. In this sense, and using the terminology explained on page 38, these activities are **other-regulated**.

What exactly *is* awareness? The concept comes from cognitivist learning theory (see page 38), which argues that, as a prerequisite for the restructuring of the learner's mental representation of the language, some degree of conscious awareness is necessary. Awareness involves at least three processes: **attention**, **noticing**, and **understanding**.

- **Attention** – learners need to be **paying attention**, i.e. they need to be on the alert – interested, involved, and curious – if they are going to notice features of the target skill.
- **Noticing** – this is more than simply paying attention. While someone is driving, they can be paying attention without noticing a great deal until a kangaroo suddenly bounds onto the road. Noticing, then, is the conscious registering of the occurrence of some event or entity. Noticing is more likely if the event or entity is somehow surprising (like the kangaroo) or if it is salient because of its frequency, size, significance, or usefulness, among other things. We also notice things if they have been previously pointed out to us. Many learners, having recently been taught a new word,

will be familiar with the experience of noticing it everywhere. The prior teaching has **primed** them to notice what before had gone unobserved.

It's also possible to notice the absence of something. For example, a learner might notice a 'hole' in their language proficiency as the result of being incapable of expressing a particular idea. They can also notice the difference between their own, novice, performance and the performance of an expert. This is called **noticing the gap**.

• **Understanding** – finally, there is no real awareness without understanding. Understanding means the recognition of a general rule or principle or pattern. This is more likely if there are several instances of the item that is being targeted for learning, so that the pattern or rule can be more easily perceived.

All these processes can be aided and supported by the presence of either a teacher or other learners. For example, the teacher can ensure a heightened degree of attention by recounting an anecdote that has a humorous or unusual outcome. She can promote noticing by incorporating into the story several instances of a narrative device, such as the sentence starter *and the X thing was …* where *X* can stand for *funny, odd, strange, weird* etc. Finally, she can support the learners' understanding of this pattern – both its form and its narrative function – by asking the learners to underline each instance of the pattern in a transcript of the anecdote.

This sequence from an intermediate coursebook is designed to raise awareness about repair strategies in casual conversation. The students have previously listened to a recording of two people talking about different types of memory.

---

## English in use
### Repair strategies

**Communication problems**

Communication problems occur even when speaking your own language, caused by:

- noise or distance: making it difficult to hear or understand
- time pressure or anxiety: making it difficult to organize your thoughts
- memory failure: forgetting the right word or not concentrating
- complexity: what you want to say is difficult to say

You can repair these problems.

1 [○3] Listen again to Lynn and Mick. What communication problems do they have? Number them 1 to 4.

| | |
|---|---|
| can't remember the right word(s) | ☐ |
| accidentally uses the wrong word | ☐ |
| has trouble forming the sentence | ☐ |
| doesn't hear / understand | ☐ |

1 **Lynn** So some time later you buy bread, and when you've done it you don't need **to restore, er to store** that memory any longer …

2 **Mick** Are there any …, are …, are any memories really permanent?

3 **Lynn** … you start to get confused.
  **Mick** Sorry?
  **Lynn** You get confused.

4 **Mick** Interconnections?
  **Lynn** Yeah, **I can't remember the right word, but** that's the problem.

2 When do we use these repair strategies?
  1 Say 'Sorry?'
  2 Say 'I can't remember / I don't know the right word', then suggest some possible words
  3 Say er / um, then say the right word
  4 Just stop, pause, and start again

3 Describe one of these. Can your partner guess what you are talking about? Use the repair strategies when you have problems.

| a job | a machine | a musical instrument | a sport |
|---|---|---|---|

---

Learners can also collaborate in the awareness-raising process, as when, in small groups, they jointly construct and rehearse a story based on picture prompts and then tell it to the members of another group, who have to put the pictures in order as they listen. The task prompts a degree of attention, and, in rehearsing the task, individual learners may 'notice the gap' between their performance and that of their peers. In attempting to fill the gap, they may be motivated to ask for assistance from their peers, and the assistance may take the form of an explanation, which in turn may aid understanding.

Of course, there is no guarantee that any of these processes will happen. But the activities that are outlined in the rest of this chapter attempt to provide optimal awareness-raising conditions and thereby maximize the chances that these learning processes will occur.

**Using recordings and transcripts**

One way to raise learners' awareness of features of spoken language is to expose them to instances of speaking and to have them study transcripts of such instances. Traditionally this has taken the form of playing learners **recordings**, either of monologue or multiparty talk (i.e. talk where several speakers are interacting), which are typically pre-scripted and performed by actors. However, the lack of spontaneity that results from being both scripted and performed means that these recordings are often only superficially representative of real spoken language. They may lack such performance effects as pause fillers, back-tracking, and repair, and they seldom display the characteristics of interactive talk, such as turn-taking, in anything but a rather idealized way. This lack of authenticity is compounded by the fact that these recordings are often designed to display a pre-selected grammar structure and are almost always simplified to ensure intelligibility.

By way of an example, here are two transcripts of the speakers talking about a similar topic. One, from J Coates' book *Men Talk* is authentic – in the sense it was unscripted and spontaneous. The other is how it might appear in a coursebook.

> Speaker 1: I went in and bought some stupid things this morning in Boots, twenty-five p, [laugh] for twenty-five p you could be as silly as you want to couldn't you? Silly aren't they? Oh what fun. Silly green nonsense. Children's bead earrings.
> Speaker 2: You got green?
> Speaker 1: I've got a green jumper which I wear in the winter
> Speaker 2: Yeah that's fine
> Speaker 1: So I thought I would. I'm – am very fond of my green jumper, silly pair of green earrings to go with it.
> Speaker 2: Why not?
> Speaker 1: It's a laugh. There was another lady there looking through all the stuff where I was and she said to me, 'Isn't it fun?' [laugh] and I said, 'Yes, only twenty-five p,' [laugh] Absurd.

Earrings 1 (authentic version)

> Speaker 1: What nice earrings!
> Speaker 2: I bought them this morning.
> Speaker 1: Where did you buy them?
> Speaker 2: I bought them in Boots.
> Speaker 1: How much did they cost?
> Speaker 2: Only twenty-five p.
> Speaker 1: What a bargain!
> Speaker 2: I'm going to wear them with my green jumper.
> Speaker 1: What a good idea!
>
> Earrings 2 (coursebook version)

The 'coursebook' dialogue is a far remove from naturally occurring speech. Its symmetrical turn distribution between speakers and its uniform utterance length are rare in casual talk among friends, where individual speakers typically hold the floor for longer periods of time and less equitably. On the other hand, *Earrings 2* is probably a lot more intelligible to learners than *Earrings 1*. The language is simplified, the turns are short, there is more redundancy in the language (i.e. language that is not strictly necessary is repeated as in *Where did you buy them? I bought them in Boots* …), and there are no asides, overlaps, interruptions, and other characteristics of unscripted talk. The authentic conversation, on the other hand, consists of a number of relatively long turns, uses ungraded language, and includes a good deal of ellipsis as well as direct reference to the immediate (unseen) situation. Because it has not been recorded in a sound studio, it is also likely to be less clearly audible than the coursebook dialogue, and thus less attractive for classroom purposes.

Pre-scripted recordings should not be dismissed totally, therefore. Apart from greater audibility, one advantage of scripting speech is that teachers can incorporate repeated examples of particular features that they want their learners to notice. For example, in *Earrings 2*, there are three instances of the construction *what* + noun phrase (*what a bargain!* etc), expressing surprise or approval. Although it makes the conversation sound a little artificial, there is more chance that the construction will be noticed here than in the first, authentic conversation, where the same construction is much less salient.

As a compromise, scripted conversations could attempt to take into account, and to incorporate, features of naturally-occurring spoken language without sacrificing their pedagogic utility. Here is a reworked version of the earrings conversation, for example:

> Speaker 1: What nice earrings!
> Speaker 2: Do you like them? Silly, aren't they? Silly green nonsense. I bought them in Boots this morning. Twenty-five p.
> Speaker 1: What a bargain! Have you got something green to go with them?
> Speaker 2: I've got a green jumper which I wear in the winter. So I thought I'd get some silly green earrings to go with it.
> Speaker 1: What fun!
> Speaker 2: I know. It's a laugh. Only twenty-five p!
>
> Earrings 3

One problem with both the authentic and non-authentic recordings that are commercially available is that they are almost exclusively of native speakers talking. It is arguable that exposure to only native speakers sets a standard of spoken interaction that is beyond either the means or the needs of most learners and that it would be more useful, and more realistic, if they had access to recordings of communicatively successful exchanges between non-native speakers.

An alternative source of spoken data is to use authentic material from, for example, radio or TV. Apart from the more formally scripted spoken texts, such as news broadcasts and documentary voice-overs, there is a lot of unscripted data, such as interviews, 'vox pop' segments (i.e. short interviews with a range of people about a particular topic, usually recorded in the street), TV talk shows, and talk-back radio, and the relatively recent phenomenon of 'reality shows' (such as *Big Brother*). The main problems with this media material (apart from questions of copyright) are, on the one hand, availability – it's not so easy to get hold of if one is teaching outside an English-speaking context – and, on the other, the level of 'insider' cultural knowledge that is necessary to make sense of such texts. Talk shows and reality shows are directed at a very specific audience and make no concessions to viewers who are not familiar with that context. Moreover, the conversations are often meandering, inconsequential, and highly colloquial. For most learners of English – especially of English as an International Language – such language is unlikely to provide a useful model. Here for example, is an extract, more or less taken at random, from Channel Four's popular reality show *Big Brother*:

| | |
|---|---|
| Gos: | Lisa, can I be rude? |
| Lisa: | You want me to move? |
| Gos: | You look better today. |
| Lisa: | Than I did yesterday? |
| Gos: | Yeah, definitely. I know you say about your make-up right, but I think you look a lot better without it. |
| Lisa: | My boyfriend always says that. |
| Gos: | It's true. |
| Lisa: | I used it as a mask yesterday, literally. I overloaded. |
| Gos: | Cameron said you looked really, really pretty without your make-up and I'm like 'yeh, really pretty man – aiiiiiiii'. I like to throw in a red herring every now and again. |
| Steph: | You causin' trouble Gos? |
| Lisa: | Not at all. He's been very complimentary. |
| Gos: | I only picked up on it 'cos Cameron said. |
| Lisa. | When I'm in here I probably won't wear any anyway. |
| Gos: | Good. And give up smoking, you're killing me! |

While the extract includes some useful interactive expressions (*Yeah, definitely. It's true. Not at all …*), it also includes examples of fairly colloquial and idiomatic usage (*I'm like, yeah, really pretty, man … I like to throw in a red herring now and again …*), plus references to shared knowledge, such as things that happened yesterday, as well as being about a topic that is probably only of interest to regular viewers (i.e. whether Lisa wears too much make-up or not).

Using scripted data, in which natural speech is 'tidied up' or simulated, such as in soap operas or extracts from films, can be a means of getting round the problem of unintelligibility. Some scriptwriters are better than others at capturing the characteristics of natural speech. Two researchers compared conversational openings and closings in both a New Zealand soap opera and coursebook dialogues, and came out in favour of the soap opera as being more representative of natural speech although still 'far from ideal'. The judicious choice of short extracts from such sources may be one way of supplementing coursebook material. But, as with other material on radio and TV, transcripts are seldom made available to the public, and this adds an extra chore for the teacher who wants to use them.

A compromise is to make our own recordings, using our teaching colleagues. For a start, teachers often have a well-developed sense of how to make adjustments to their speech that favour intelligibility without sacrificing authenticity. The following is a transcript of a recording a teacher made, minutes before a lesson, using teachers recruited from the staffroom, and with the instruction, 'Compliment Jackie on her earrings, and try to include an example of *what a …* . Jackie, you respond, maybe saying where you got them'.

A: I really like your earrings. Where did you get them?
B: I got them in a little shop in Figueras, actually.
A: They really go with your outfit.
B: Cheers.
A: How much were they?
B: Three euros, I think.
A: Cor, what a bargain.

Notice that, although the language is kept within the bounds of comprehensibility of most intermediate learners, it still manages to include a number of features of spoken English, including the tails *actually* and *I think*, and the evaluative language *really*, *cheers*, and *cor*.

The recording is one thing, but the transcript is another. Coursebook recordings are now always accompanied by a transcription, which is usually located in a section at the back of the book. Making one's own transcript of a homemade recording can be a lengthy process, but there is no better way of getting to know the material and of discovering features that might initially have been overlooked. This is a powerful argument for getting the learners themselves to do the transcribing: it increases the chances of their **noticing** features of the data as well as helping develop their listening skills in general.

Linguists observe a number of conventions when making transcriptions of naturally-occurring talk, such as marking pause length and signalling overlaps (i.e. where two speakers are speaking at once). Most of this 'notation' will serve little pedagogic use, although, for some purposes, marking stressed words may be helpful. It is important, however, not to edit out too many of the performance effects, such as hesitations, repetitions, and false starts. Showing learners that even proficient speakers have to make real-time adjustments, and showing them *how* they make these adjustments, can only be helpful in the long run.

Whatever way the transcript is made, it is essential that a transcript be available for study purposes at some stage of the teaching sequence. No matter how many times learners are replayed a recording, there will be features of it that elude them until they see them written down. And even if they have reconstructed the text word for word, it will still be satisfying to match their mental representation of the text with the written form. Also, listening to the recording while at the same time reading it silently can help reinforce sound–spelling connections. Finally, it is often easier for the teacher to draw attention to patterns and regularities by reference to the written text than by simply trying to isolate them on a recording.

### A basic procedure

Having obtained recorded data, how can the teacher put it to good practical use? There are a number of ways of using recorded speech data and their accompanying transcripts, but we can start with a basic procedure for staging the use of recordings. (Note that the use of the term *recording* below is shorthand for whatever form of recording is chosen, whether audiocassette, video, CD, DVD etc)

 **Activate background knowledge** – depending on the difficulty of the content, it may help to establish the topic and/or the context of the speech event: this will make the subsequent tasks easier. If, for example, the speakers on the recording are comparing two different models of bicycle, it will help the learners' listening load if they first brainstorm vocabulary related to bicycles (e.g. *tyres, gears, brakes, saddle, frame* etc). This both situates them, mentally, in terms of the topic and is a way of dealing with unfamiliar vocabulary items that are likely to occur. (The teacher can introduce items that the learners don't come up with but which occur in the recording.) A related idea is to ask the learners to improvise a conversation on the same topic themselves, before playing them the recording.

**Check gist** – play the extract, or an initial segment of it, and ask general gist questions. For example, 'Who is talking to whom about what, and why?' Note that establishing the gist of what is going on is a prerequisite for all of the activities that follow. The advantages of video material in terms of providing contextual information should be obvious, but even video can't provide all the details, such as the topic of the conversation. Repeated listenings may be necessary, with learners noting key words and comparing in pairs or small groups, before a general consensus on the gist can be established.

 **Check register** – related to the above, it is often important to establish the register variables, particularly the **tenor** of the speech situation (see page 19), as these will have an impact on certain language choices, such as the degree of formality involved. Check, therefore, that the learners are clear as to the relationship between speakers, their relative rank, and/or social distance.

 **Check details** – depending to what extent the teacher wants to achieve **zero uncertainty** – that is, 100% comprehension of the text on the part of all learners – the learners may need to be set further, more probing, tasks, such as a table to complete, a grid to fill, or multiple choice questions to answer. The recording should be replayed as many times as necessary for learners to complete these tasks. Learners should also be given the opportunity to consult each other.

 **Listen and read** – hand out the transcript (assuming one is available; alternatively, learners can produce their own transcript at this stage, even if only of a part of the recording). Replay the recording while learners read silently.

 **Resolve doubts** – learners should be given the opportunity to ask about any residual doubts or problems they have about the text. In a monolingual class, this may involve translating items that remain obscure or allowing learners to consult dictionaries.

 **Focus on language features** – by now the learners should be sufficiently familiar with the text to have a basis for 'guided noticing' of selected features. This can involve the following procedures:

- *identifying*, e.g. underline, or circle, in the transcript examples of evaluative language.
- *counting*, e.g. count the number of times the speakers say *you know* and *I mean*.
- *classifying*, e.g. identify and classify the different discourse markers.
- *matching*, e.g. match idiomatic expressions in the text with their synonyms on a list.
- *connecting*, e.g. connect the pronouns in the text with their referents (i.e. the words they refer to).
- *comparing and contrasting*, e.g. compare these two versions of the same conversation and identify any differences.

An alternative way of guiding noticing is to provide a transcript that is either incomplete or in some way different from the actual recording. For example:

- Listen to the recording again and fill in the gaps in the transcript. (The gaps can represent all the discourse markers, for example.)
- Listen to the recording again and spot any differences in the transcript. (The difference could be that none of the backchannel devices (e.g. *uh-huh, really? how awful*) are included in the transcript.)

The above procedure is not meant to be prescriptive and can be adapted according to the demands of the listening text itself, and to the level and needs of the learners. But one important principle should normally be observed: that learners need to have a basic understanding of the text before they embark on close study of its language features.

**Focusing on selected language features**

Here are some further ideas, using recordings and their transcripts, for focusing on selected language features. They have been organized top-down from the more global type features to the more discrete type (as described in Chapter 2):

 **Focus on organization** – to sensitize learners to the features of spoken genres that may be unfamiliar to them, such as giving business presentations or presenting conference papers, use the transcript to identify the **macro-structure** of the genre. This means identifying each stage in the sequence, e.g. *introduction, problem, possible solution 1, drawbacks, possible solution 2, drawbacks, possible solution 3, advantages, conclusion.* The learners can either be given the names of the stages and asked to match them to sections of the text or to provide their own categorization. A logical follow-up activity would be to identify the expressions that are used to signal the onset of the different stages. (For more on the structure of presentations, see page 94.)

 **Focus on sociocultural rules** – although we have emphasized the dangers, difficulties, and possible irrelevance of teaching learners how to behave according to the cultural norms of the target language society, it may be the case that, for certain learners, some cultural awareness-raising may be recommended. Learners who are going to visit, or study in, a specific English-speaking culture and who have expressed apprehension at the prospect of offending their hosts, may benefit from some preparation. One way of doing this is to prepare two versions of a cross-cultural encounter – one of which is successful in that no offence or embarrassment is caused – and one of which is not successful. Possible scenarios might include a visit to a family's home for a meal or the buying of a round of drinks in a pub. Care should be taken, however, that the participants in the encounter are not caricatured in any stereotypical way. Learners listen to the two scenarios, compare them, discuss what went wrong in the unsuccessful encounter, and suggest ways of repairing it. They could also talk about how such an encounter might be conducted in their own culture.

Here on the left is a coursebook activity that is aimed at raising awareness about the appropriacy of particular topics in casual conversation.

### Speaking: Small talk

**1** Imagine you are at a formal party with people whom you are meeting for the first time. Which of the subjects below do you think are appropriate as topics for conversation in (a) your own country and (b) Britain? Complete the table below, adding any comments if you wish.

| Topic | Own country | Britain |
|---|---|---|
| today's weather | | |
| your opinions about marriage | | |
| your religious beliefs | | |
| how you got to the party | | |
| your political views | | |
| a recent sporting event | | |
| the food and drink at the party | | |
| your salary | | |
| a TV programme you saw last night | | |
| the latest political crisis | | |
| the attractiveness of your host | | |
| a neighbour's sudden death | | |
| some physical symptoms you've got | | |

**Focus on topic shift** – make (or choose) a recording where the topic of conversation changes at least three times. One way of doing this is to set up a situation in which two or three people are comparing experiences of living in or visiting a particular country. The topics can cover such things as the weather, the food, the people, getting around, the sights, or the language. Ideally, the conversation should not be scripted in advance so as to catch the natural way that intonation signals new topics. Alternatively, ask three or four colleagues to improvise a conversation based around a list of pre-selected topics, such as something on TV last night, a friend's wedding, or a great new restaurant. Ask the learners, first, to list the topics they hear or to tick topics from a list. Then replay the recording and ask them to signal (e.g. by raising their hands) whenever a topic changes. Finally, ask them to note down any language associated with these topic shifts, such as *by the way …*, *that reminds me …*, *speaking of which …*, *well, …* .

 **Focus on performance effects** – ask learners to use a transcript to identify features of unscripted talk that result from its real-time construction, for example, pause fillers, repairs, production strategies etc (see page 21). Ask them how they would translate these features into their first language. Alternatively, record from television or radio some speakers talking in the learners' L1 (assuming a monolingual class), and ask them how they would render the pause fillers, repairs etc, in English. This is a way of highlighting those universal features of conversation that result from its real-time, jointly constructed nature. Here, for example, is a sequence of activities designed to raise awareness about fillers:

> In everyday conversation, people often use 'fillers' such as *um*, *well* and *sort of*. Can you think of any others?
> You will hear three people talking about smoking. Note down the fillers the speakers use. Why do you think they use them? How necessary do you think they are?
>
> 1  Well, I do like it, I mean really I know I shouldn't, but um, you know how it is, if you have one and you want another it's um, it's a bit difficult to stop, really.
>
> 2  I think it's a really um disgusting habit, really, and you know, you know if you're um in a restaurant or something and people start smoking, I think it's disgusting, basically, I think it's really awful.
>
> 3  Yeah, well I've been smoking now for, ooh I don't know, about 30 years or so I suppose, and I'm kind of smoking one year and kind of giving up the next, and um actually it's been going on like that for ages and um you know when I, when I give up I just put on all this weight. So I kind of give up, and then I get very depressed because I'm overweight, so I kind of um, so I take it up again.

**Focus on communication strategies** – script or improvise some conversations where speakers use a variety of communication strategies to achieve their goal. One possible situation is a succession of customers in a hardware shop, each of whom is buying an item whose name they don't know. Another is simply having people describe things, and the learners choose the item from a set or pictures. Here is an example from a coursebook:

SPEAKER 1: Well, it's ... it's that stuff you need to put two different pieces together. For instance, two pieces of paper. You put that stuff on one bit of paper and stick the other paper on top of it, for example. Or, you can do that with leather as well, if your shoe gets broken, or you can do that with wood, and things like that.

SPEAKER 2: It's a piece of material. Um ... it's a square and it's soft and you use it to ... after a bath for drying yourself when you are wet.

SPEAKER 3: It looks like little pieces of wood, very thin little pieces all in a box and, er ... at the tip there's a ... they are either black or red and it's something you use to light a fire or anything like that.

SPEAKER 4: Er ... I want ... you put it on when it's hot and you buy it in a bottle, a plastic bottle and you put it on your body and it protects you from the sun.

SPEAKER 5: It's a machine for cleaning. You have a tube and it, er ... it sucks the dust. It's a machine for cleaning the carpet or the floor.

2  Listen to people describing five of the objects in the pictures, which they don't know the English word for. Write the name of the object each speaker describes.

Speaker 1 _____ Speaker 2 _____ Speaker 3 _____
Speaker 4 _____ Speaker 5 _____

 **Focus on speech acts** – script or improvise a conversation which involves a number of speech acts, for example, a compliment, a response to a compliment, an invitation, an acceptance, a suggestion, a request, an apology-plus-refusal-plus-excuse, a promise. Here is a conversation that follows that model:

Al: Hey, Barry, what a great tie!
Barry: Thanks. Actually, I've had it for ages, but I never wear it.
Al: It suits you. Listen, Barry, I was thinking, do you fancy lunch together some time this week?
Barry: That'd be nice. What about Friday?
Al: Perfect. Do you mind if I ask Jackie?
Barry: Well, actually, I'm sorry Al, I'd rather you didn't. It's just that Jackie doesn't know I'm back, and ...
Al: OK. I understand. I won't tell her, I promise.

Write up the list of speech acts in a jumbled order, and ask learners to match each speech act with its realization. Then ask them to identify the words or formulaic expression that are the indicators of each speech act. For example *what a* [positive adjective + noun] = compliment; *what about* [+ noun]? = suggestion etc. As a follow-up, learners can attempt to script, rehearse, and perform their own dialogues using these formulas.

Asking learners to categorize speech acts is another way of raising awareness as to their meaning and use. In the following activity, learners first match short dialogues to a picture and then categorize a variety of speech acts relating to the macro-function of 'getting people to do things':

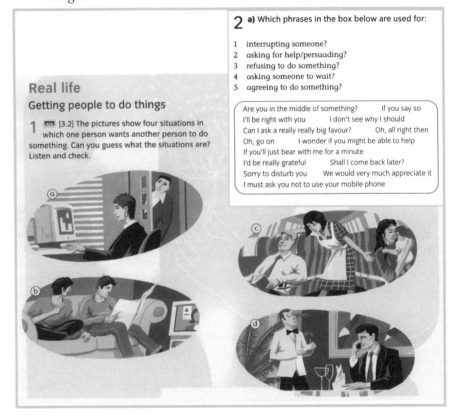

**2 a)** Which phrases in the box below are used for:

1  interrupting someone?
2  asking for help/persuading?
3  refusing to do something?
4  asking someone to wait?
5  agreeing to do something?

Are you in the middle of something?    If you say so
I'll be right with you    I don't see why I should
Can I ask a really really big favour?    Oh, all right then
Oh, go on    I wonder if you might be able to help
If you'll just bear with me for a minute
I'd be really grateful    Shall I come back later?
Sorry to disturb you    We would very much appreciate it
I must ask you not to use your mobile phone

## Real life

### Getting people to do things

1  [3.2] The pictures show four situations in which one person wants another person to do something. Can you guess what the situations are? Listen and check.

**Focus on discourse markers** – script or improvise a conversation that includes some common discourse markers such as *well, so, oh, I mean, right*, and *anyway*. As suggested above, leave these out of the transcript and ask learners to restore them, checking with the recording to see if they are right. Alternatively, make two versions of a conversation, one with the discourse markers and one without. Before handing out the transcript, ask learners if they notice any difference. Then play them the two conversations again while they read the transcript. Having established the difference, ask them to comment on what effect the discourse markers have. A list of common discourse markers and their meanings may be useful at this point: there is one on page 9.

 **Focus on features of spoken grammar** – the compare-and-contrast approach, outlined in the previous section, can also be applied to the highlighting of features of spoken grammar, such as **ellipsis**, **heads** and **tails**, **repetition**, and the clause-by-clause, rather than sentence-by-sentence construction. For example, learners can listen to two versions of the same conversation, such as *Earrings 1* and *Earrings 2* on pages 43 and 44, and attempt to identify differences before studying a transcript. Alternatively, they could compare a written version of, say, a narrative, with its spoken equivalent. Here, for example, is the story about kedgeree (in Chapter 1) retold as a written narrative.

> Once, when I was at school, our domestic science teacher told us we would be making kedgeree. Kedgeree is an old-fashioned colonial dish and hardly appropriate for a comprehensive school. Nevertheless, we were asked to bring a pound of fish to school the following week. When I told my mother, she refused, on the grounds that we didn't like kedgeree. As a result, I had to take a note to the teacher, which said that my mother wouldn't allow me to make kedgeree since the family didn't like it. It was humiliating to have to sit and watch as the other girls made it.

Some of the more obvious differences between this version and the spoken one are:

- the use of complete sentences
- the use of subordinate clauses, e.g. *when I was at school*
- the use of indirect speech (*she refused …*)
- the written narrative is more explicit (*Kedgeree is an old-fashioned colonial dish …*)
- the use of passive constructions (*we were asked …*)
- the use of more formal cohesive devices (*Nevertheless, As a result …*)
- the use of more formal ways of expressing appraisal (*humiliating*, rather than *awful*)

On page 54 is a sequence of activities designed to raise awareness about the use of ellipsis in spoken language.

 **Focus on vocabulary** – use a transcript of naturally occurring talk, preferably by proficient learners, to demonstrate the high proportion of high-frequency vocabulary that is characteristic of spoken language. Ask learners to do a count of the 'top band' words, using a dictionary such as the *Longman Dictionary of Contemporary English*, in which word frequency is indicated. See page 35 for an example of how this is done.

It can also be instructive to ask learners to compare the **lexical density** of spoken language with written language. Lexical density is a measure of the proportion of **content words** in a text. Content words –

## A  Introduction

**1**  Look at these extracts from conversations.

■  Mark places where you feel words may be missing, write a fuller version of
   the sentences you have marked, and compare the two versions. ☞

a)  [Jim is telling Ken what route he took in his car to get to Ken's house. Mistham
    is the name of a small town.]
    Jim:  And I came over by Mistham, by the reservoirs.
    Ken:  Oh, by Mistham, over the top, nice route.
    Jim:  Colours are pleasant, aren't they?
    Ken:  Yes.
    Jim:  Nice run, that.

b)  [Two brothers are talking.]
    Matt:     Are you late?
    Roman:  Yes, really late.
    Matt:     What time's the film start?
    Roman:  Seven-thirty.
    Matt:     You've got half-an-hour.
    Roman:  Any chance of a lift in your car?

c)  [Paul is cooking rice in a microwave oven. Ingrid is watching him.]
    Ingrid:  Didn't know you used boiling water.
    Paul:    They reckon it's quicker.

**2**  Would each of the following be acceptable in formal situations? If not, why not?

a)  Are you ready yet? / You ready yet?
b)  Too late. / It is too late.
c)  Fine, thanks. / I'm fine, thanks.
d)  I'm not sure really. / Not sure really.
e)  Is she French? Yes, she's French. / Is she French? Yes, French.

as opposed to function words – are words that carry a high information
load, such as nouns, adjectives, the adverbs that end in *-ly*, and verbs
(but not auxiliary or modal verbs). The measure of lexical density is the
number of content words as a percentage of the total number of words.
As a rule, spoken language is less dense than written language. This is
because speech consists of a higher proportion of the 'small words' of
the language – that is, pronouns, discourse markers, conjunctions, and
auxiliary verbs. So, the written version of the kedgeree story (above)
has a lexical density of 47%, as opposed to its spoken version, which
has a density of only 38%.

   One feature of spoken language that is primarily lexical is the use of
**vague language**. The two exercises on page 55 focus on the use of the
indefinite pronouns *something* and *anything*, and on the suffix *-ish*, to
express vagueness.

## 6 | ... or something/... or anything

**Look at these two examples:**

My dad thought I was a pick-pocket or a drug addict or something.

There was no hot water or showers or anything!

**Phrases with or something/or anything are common in spoken English when we want to be vague. Complete these sentences with the language in the box below.**

> or something like that    food or anything
> showers or anything    a bit of wire or something
> a hammer or something

1. He managed to get the lock to work by using
   . . . . . . . . . . . . . . . . . . . .  .

2. The campsite was horrible. There were no proper
   toilets or . . . . . . . . . . . . . . . . . . . . .  .

3. They must have broken into the car with
   . . . . . . . . . . . . . . . . . . . . . They did a lot of damage.

4. I didn't really see the registration number, but I'm
   sure it started TKP . . . . . . . . . . . . . . . . . . .  .

5. We flew on one of those budget airlines. There were
   no drinks or . . . . . . . . . . . . . . . . . . . . .  .

> For more information on how to use these structures,
> see G19.

## 7 | -ish

**Adding -ish to an adjective or number is a common way of being less precise.**

He's about forty-ish.

Her hair is a sort of reddish brown.

**Complete the sentences below with the words in the box.**

> seven-ish    yellow-ish    purple-ish
> long-ish    tall-ish    sixty-ish

1. He's not retired yet, but I'm sure he's about
   . . . . . . . . . . .  .

2. When you get malaria, your skin turns a sort of
   . . . . . . . . . . colour.

3. I think we'll have to get the train about . . . . . . . . . . to
   get there in time for eight.

4. Although it was red wine, it was a kind of deep
   . . . . . . . . . . colour.

5. Eva's the one with . . . . . . . . . . dark hair.

6. You'll recognise him. He's a sort of . . . . . . . . . . version
   of Charlie Chaplin without the moustache.

**Focus on lexical chunks** – chunks can consist of such things as common **collocations** (*the fast track, fast asleep*), **word pairs** (*fast and furious, hard and fast rules*), and **idioms**, **phrasal verbs**, and **catchphrases** (*make something fast, life in the fast lane, play fast and loose*). On page 23, we identified the lexical chunks in a segment of authentic conversation. The same procedure can be done by learners, using a transcript and cross-checking by means of a good learner's dictionary. Ask them to go through the text, underlining potential chunks, and then to consult the dictionary to check their intuitions. Even if the item that learners have identified as a possible chunk is not in fact listed as such, the search may yield other useful idioms and expressions. For example, in the transcript of *Earrings 1*, on page 43, the following two expressions occur, each a potential chunk: *what fun* and *it's a laugh*. The CD for the *Longman Dictionary of Contemporary English* does not include *what fun* in its phrase bank, presumably because it is not significantly frequent. But it does have the following very useful chunks: *for fun, fun and games, great fun, it's no fun, join in the fun, just for the fun of it*, and *sounds like fun*. Under the entry for *laugh*, *it's a* [adjective] *laugh* is included, along with *that's a laugh, for laughs, had a good laugh*, and *be a laugh a minute*.

**Focus on stress and intonation** – recordings can be used to highlight the way stress and intonation are used to signal new or important information, to segment speech into meaningful chunks, and to signal the connections between chunks. For example, a small section of the recording can be played as many times as necessary for learners to mark the stressed words on the transcript. This is particularly useful if there are instances of contrastive stress, as in:

> I never met Lisa's brother but I met her SISTER.
>
> I said we'd meet at FIVE, not six.
>
> **A:** What do you do?
> **B:** I'm a nurse. What do YOU do?

Alternatively, learners can first read the transcript and try to predict the stress, before hearing the recording.

 Another technique for sensitizing learners to the contrastive use of stress is to record a number of sentences that are the same in every particular except for the placement of stress. Learners listen and choose, from a set of written alternatives, the most likely continuation for each sentence. So, for example, they hear:

> Terry's not meeting MARION tonight.

And they choose from:

> **1** Kim's meeting her.
> **2** He's meeting her tomorrow night.
> **3** He's meeting Sharon.

Then they hear:

> TERRY'S not meeting Marion tonight.

And they choose again.

 Transcripts can also be used to divide the text up into 'runs' – that is, any sequence of words or syllables between pauses. Identifying runs, and the prominent stress within each run, is useful preparation for reading aloud (to be dealt with in the following chapter).

 Recordings can also be used to highlight the use of intonation to signal both the introduction of a new topic (typically marked by a significant rise in pitch) and the completion of a speaker turn (typically marked by a paratone, see page 25). Recognizing paratones may be a useful interactive skill, since knowing when to bid for a turn depends on knowing when the present floor-holder has come to the end of their turn. As an example activity, the recording of an unscripted conversation can be stopped at strategic moments and the learners asked, *Has he/she finished yet?*

Other areas of intonation are less amenable to direct instruction. Asking learners to identify pitch direction, for example, is notoriously difficult. The question 'Is the voice going up or down here?' is one that even experts have trouble with and is best avoided.

**Using live listening**

Recordings allow learners exposure to a range of accents and voice types and, more importantly, to multiparty talk. They also allow repeated replayings and hence close analysis of language features, and, because recordings can be made in advance, transcripts, too, can be prepared in advance. But apart from these advantages, recordings are of limited usefulness. The often poor sound quality and their 'disembodied' nature makes them a less than ideal medium for the development of speaking skills.

Exposure to speech needn't be mediated only by recordings, of course. A better but perhaps less exploited alternative is the teacher. **Live listening**, i.e. listening to the teacher or a guest speaker, has the particular advantage of interactivity: the teacher can adjust her talk according to her perception of the learners' level of understanding, and the learners can interact to ask questions, clarify details, and solicit repeats, as well as simply signal they are understanding (through backchannel devices, for example). Live listening does not involve the distractions of technology, such as finding the place on the recording, is more audible, and is, of course, supported by helpful paralinguistic information such as that supplied by gesture and facial expression. Finally, the intrinsic interest generated by listening to someone who is known to the learners, and physically present, is a much more powerful motivator than listening to a disembodied stranger.

How can these advantages be best exploited in order to raise awareness of features of spoken language? One technique that works well is to combine the advantages of live listening with those of recorded listening, and make a recording while 'speaking live'. This requires only a cassette recorder, preferably a personal stereo, to record with and a classroom cassette player for playback purposes. Here, for example, is a description of a lesson I observed where this technique was used:

---

The teacher introduced the topic of his brother by showing a family photograph. The students were invited to ask one or two questions and established the brother's name, job, and so on. The teacher then announced that he was going to tell the class a story about his brother, and at this point he switched on the portable cassette recorder he was holding. He told the story using natural but uncomplicated language (there was no script) and occasionally stopped to check understanding (e.g. 'Do you know where Denver is?') or to explain a term ('*Hitchhiking* is when you travel by getting free rides in other people's cars … '). During the telling of the story he used a number of time and sequencing expressions, such as *once …* , *eventually …* , *all of a sudden …* , as well as other story-telling devices, such as *so there he was, …* and *well, to cut a long story short …* , and some evaluative language, such as *petrified, scared stiff, incredible,* and *totally amazed*. At the end of the story, which took about two minutes to tell, the students were invited to ask questions. Some clarification of details as well as answers to questions about the aftermath of the story were necessary.

Then the teacher asked the learners if they could remember any of the time and sequencing expressions he had used. One student suggested *suddenly*. Another remembered *then*. Having pricked their curiosity, he transferred

Continues …

---

> the tape to the classroom cassette player and played the recording, the instruction being to note down any time and sequencing expressions. These were checked and written on the board. The same procedure was used for the story-telling devices and the evaluative language. By now the students were sufficiently familiar with the story to tell it to each other in pairs, while attempting to incorporate the language they had just been focusing on. Finally, they volunteered similar stories they had either experienced or heard about.

This technique can be used to focus on any of the aspects of spoken language that were outlined in the previous section, such as overall organization, the use of discourse markers, features of spoken grammar, lexical chunks, and stress and intonation. It requires of the teacher only the ability to incorporate these features into the actual telling. Preparing notes in advance may help, but it is important that the telling should be unscripted so that the rhythms and performance effects of natural speech are realistically represented.

**Using noticing-the-gap activities**

Apart from noticing features of the input that they are exposed to, learners can get important messages about their current state of proficiency by attending to their own output, and by making comparisons between their output and that of others. Activities aimed at raising awareness of the difference between the learner's current competence and the target competence are called **noticing-the-gap activities**. Again, the teacher can play an important role here, in guiding the learner to notice certain gaps. However, the teacher is not always the best judge of the learner's current 'state of readiness'. There is some evidence to suggest that learners will only notice certain features of the L2 when they have reached the developmental stage in which they are ready to notice them. So, probably the most effective gap noticing is that which is initiated by the learners themselves. The researcher Keith Johnson makes this point, using an analogy with learning to ride a horse:

> I was having problems doing a good trot, and the teacher was demonstrating what it should look like. During her demonstration, I noticed something about the position of her legs which she had never drawn my attention to; it was not on her 'teaching programme'. Once I held my legs in the same position, several of the things which I was getting wrong and which she *had* drawn my attention to suddenly became right. In that situation I was learning something she had not set out to teach. Language teachers may find in their experience similar examples of where 'point learned' is at odds with 'intended teaching point'.

This suggests that, in the learning of at least some aspects of a skill such as speaking, learners may benefit from first 'having a go' and then observing a skilled practitioner performing the same task. The term **task** is used intentionally here since the cycle of **perform – observe – re-perform** is the basis of the **task-based approach** to language learning. How does this work in practice? Here are some classroom scenarios:

The teacher sets up the context for a speech event – for example, two people fixing a date to meet or someone returning a faulty item to a store. Learners are paired off and attempt to perform the task, using whatever linguistic means they have available. They then listen to a recording – or watch a video – of two 'expert speakers' performing the same task. Jane Willis, in her book *A Framework for Task-Based Learning*, offers the following advice when playing recordings of skilled speakers performing a task learners have just done themselves:

- Introduce the speakers on the cassette.
- Make sure the students realize the speakers are doing a similar task to the one they will do or have done.
- Make sure they know that you don't expect them to understand everything. Tell them it might sound difficult to start with, but you'll play it several times.
- Make sure students know why they're listening each time you play the recording.

Having listened to the task being performed, learners should then have the chance of studying a transcript of the recording. They can be asked to note any features, such as useful expressions, that they would like to incorporate into a re-performance of the original task. Some focused work on these features may be advisable. For example, they could first write a conversation, incorporating these features, before attempting the improvised re-performance.

 Learners perform a monologic speaking task, e.g. describing the organizational structure of their company, telling an anecdote, or simply chatting about their weekend. The teacher listens and then **reformulates** the learner's monologue. That is, the teacher repeats back to the learner the gist of the learner's spoken text, putting it into her own words, and maybe commenting on any changes she has made. The process is well captured in this description by Earl Stevick:

> Another of my favourite techniques is to tell something to a speaker of the language and have that person tell the same thing back to me in correct, natural form. I then tell the same thing again, bearing in mind the way in which I have just heard it [i.e. having noticed the gap]. This cycle can repeat itself two or three times ... An essential feature of this technique is that the text we are swapping back and forth originates with me, so that I control the content ... .

Obviously, this technique works best in a 1-to-1 situation, but it's not impossible to set up in a classroom: the teacher can work with individuals while the rest of the class is rehearsing their monologue in pairs or small groups.

A variant of this activity that works well with beginners is to allow the learner to perform the task in their L1, which the teacher then re-casts into the L2. Obviously, this technique assumes that the teacher is a proficient speaker of both languages, and even then, it will require a fair bit of thinking on the spot.

At some stage of the process, it would be useful to record both the learner's monologue and the teacher's reformulation of it, so that the learner can study the differences between the two texts at their leisure.

 Learners enact a scenario in pairs or small groups, but this time they are recorded – either audio or video – while they are doing it. To be fair, they should be given a chance to rehearse first, as being recorded can be quite threatening. However, it is important that the scenario be enacted without reference to a script, even if a script was used in the rehearsal stage. The recording is then played back, and learners are given a chance to evaluate it. Again, it is less threatening if this takes the form of self-evaluation, rather than peer-evaluation, and some kind of rubric could be provided which directs attention to positive features as much as negative ones. For example:

> Listen to yourself on tape and note:
>   two or three things you succeeded in doing
>   two or three things you'd like to do better next time

Having assessed themselves, learners could compare their assessments with their classmates.

Here, for example, is how one student evaluated her performance after listening to it on tape:

> +I think that my fluencie is OK.
> −My grammar is not good because sometimes I think quicker as I speak.
> −My pronunciation is too Spanish specially in past tenses, it's difficult verb's pronunciation

 A further variation is that – having been recorded – learners work together to write their own transcript. (If the activity was a monologue, the transcript writing is done individually.) While the process of transcript writing is time-consuming, it is highly productive in terms of its awareness-raising potential. Learners are able to identify many of their own errors themselves and show gains in the accuracy and complexity of their language when they come to repeat the task. Tony Lynch calls this process 'proof-listening' (by analogy with proofreading). In Lynch's version, the learners are recorded performing a task in pairs, and together they then make a transcription (Transcript 1), working together with a single cassette recorder. They then edit this transcription, that is, they make corrections and improvements. This second transcript (Transcript 2) is submitted to the teacher, who makes any additional changes (Transcript 3). The students then compare Transcripts 2 and 3 and discuss with the teacher any points they thought were important or interesting. Lynch notes that the students showed no signs of boredom or frustration with the transcribing process.

Another researcher, Paul Mennin, describes how he used this technique to prepare groups of Japanese learners to make joint oral presentations:

> Two weeks before the scheduled final presentation, each group of three students performed a private rehearsal, with me as the only listener. The rehearsals lasted approximately 20 minutes and were recorded. These rehearsals, like the final presentations, were given without the use of scripts, though students were allowed to use small cue cards. I asked the students to transcribe a five-minute segment, which included equal contributions from each of them. They first of all transcribed the extract 'warts and all', including any errors that they made. They produced a typed transcript with double spacing, and made their own corrections in red pen. When they were finished, I took the copy and indicated any corrections or improvements that they had missed. This completed the task, and the paper was returned to them one week before they were due to give the final presentation.

In the final presentations, there was a noticeable improvement in a number of language features, particularly in the use of articles and prepositions, as well as in the overall organization of the content.

 A technique that is less labour-intensive than transcribing is **minuting**. Minuting a task, a conversation, or even a whole lesson, means making a written record of what happened, as when one *minutes* a meeting. The teacher can thereby include in the minutes any useful language that arose or can recast what learners said to make it sound more idiomatic. Here, for example, is how a teacher in a college in Manchester minuted a part of a lesson:

> We started the class by talking about how people had spent their weekends and finding out a bit more information about where people lived. We discovered that Vicky lived with a Chinese family, Victor lived with a Malaysian woman who made sure he never went hungry, and Vincent lived with some Chinese students (who all rely on him whenever they have to get in touch with the landlord, the utilities companies etc). When Vincent told us that he had lived with a host family prior to living with his friends but that he had left because his **landlady** was **stingy**, Vicky wanted to check the meaning of **landlady**. This was a good opportunity to practise the skill of explaining unknown vocabulary. Vincent gave a good dictionary definition, but, perhaps unsurprisingly, Vicky remained in the dark. I offered the advice, '**Always build on what your listener already knows when you are trying to explain new information.**' …

The learners, too, can be asked to reflect on the lesson and to recall anything that they consciously noted. Another teacher, in Italy, describes how she sets this up:

> Occasionally, I ask students to reflect on a lesson at the end, and to write down a personal note (for their eyes only), by dictating a few questions, such as, 'something someone said that surprised or interested you', 'a word or expression you particularly liked', 'how you felt during the lesson', and perhaps a question to focus on a particular language item that came up.

**Conclusions**

In this chapter we have looked at ways of raising learners' awareness about features of speaking. This can be done through exposure to samples of speech that are:

- audio-recorded (either scripted, semi-scripted, or authentic).
- 'live', e.g. in the form of teacher-talk.

Awareness can also be enhanced when learners notice the gap between what they can do and what a skilled practitioner can do. One way of engineering this is to adopt a task-based instructional cycle:

- students perform a speaking task to the best of their current ability.
- they then observe skilled practitioners performing the same task, and they note features they would like to incorporate.
- they re-perform the original task (or a similar one), attempting to incorporate the targeted features.

Other 'noticing-the-gap' techniques involve the reformulating, transcribing, and minuting of learner output.

**Looking ahead**

So far we have dealt with the issue of how to help learners fill gaps in their knowledge, with regard to speaking. But equally important is that the new-found knowledge is smoothly integrated into their existing language competence. That is, the knowledge needs to be appropriated so that it is available for use. To address this issue we will look at what we will call appropriation activities.

# 5 Appropriation activities

- **Appropriation: practised control**
- **Drilling and chants**
- **Writing tasks**
- **Reading aloud**
- **Assisted performance and scaffolding**
- **Dialogues**
- **Communicative tasks**
- **Task repetition**

**Appropriation: practised control**

In Chapter 3, the process of achieving expertise in a skill – such as speaking – was outlined as having at least three stages: awareness, appropriation, and autonomy.

The term *appropriation*, rather than either *controlled practice* or *restructuring*, is used for the second stage because it captures better the sense that learning a skill is not simply a behaviour (like practice) or a mental process (like restructuring), but one of collaborative construction. Over time, and through social interaction, the skill, which is first 'other-regulated', becomes 'self-regulated'. Central to the notion of a transfer of control is the idea that aspects of the skill are appropriated. Appropriation has connotations of taking over the ownership of something, of 'making something one's own'.

In fact, rather than talk of controlled practice, it may be more helpful to talk about **practised control**. Controlled practice is repetitive practice of language items in conditions where the possibility of making mistakes is minimized. Typically this takes the form of drilling. Practised control, on the other hand, involves demonstrating progressive control of a skill where the possibility of making mistakes is ever-present, but where support is always at hand. To use the analogy of learning to ride a bicycle, it is like being allowed to pedal freely, but with someone running along right behind, just in case. In practised control, control (or self-regulation) is the objective of the practice, whereas in controlled practice, control is simply the condition under which practice takes place.

**Drilling and chants**

Gaining control of the speaking skill involves practising that control. But the notion of practised control need not rule out the value of some mechanical and repetitive practice activities of the type traditionally associated with drilling. Drilling – that is imitating and repeating words, phrases, and even whole utterances – may in fact be a useful *noticing* technique, since it draws attention to material that learners might not otherwise have registered. Thus, after learners have listened to a taped dialogue, and studied the transcript, the teacher can isolate specific phrases or utterances and ask learners to repeat them. The effect of repeating them is bound to make them more salient. However, if *all* the dialogue were drilled, this benefit would be lost.

Drilling may also function to move new items from working memory into long-term memory, just as we tend to memorize new pin codes or telephone numbers by repeating them a number of times.

Another argument often used in favour of drilling is that it provides a means of gaining articulatory control over language – of 'getting your tongue round it'. This is probably more useful when learners are already familiar with an item – when they have already 'got their minds round it' – but are still having trouble producing the item fluidly. That is to say, drilling acts as a kind of fine tuning for articulation, rather than as a learning technique in itself. This is likely to be particularly useful in gaining control of short, functional chunks and their associated intonation patterns, such as these discourse markers:

| by the way | that reminds me | as I was saying |
|---|---|---|
| while I remember | before I forget | talking of which |

Or these sentence starters:

| Do you mind if I … ? | The thing is, … | Do you happen to know …? |
|---|---|---|
| Do you think you could … ? | Would it be OK if I … ? | |

Or social formulas and useful expressions:

| How do you do? | See you later. | Just looking, thanks. |
|---|---|---|
| Can I take a message? | How do you spell that? | |

Or catchphrases and idiomatic phrases:

| Better late than never. | Long time no see. | Look who's talking. |
|---|---|---|
| It's on the tip of my tongue. | The sooner the better. | |

By both memorizing these chunks and gaining control over their fluent articulation, learners are increasing their fluency store. As we saw in Chapter 1, fluency is the capacity to string long runs together, with appropriately placed pausing. This in turn is partly a function of having a store of memorized phrases, or chunks, that act as 'islands of reliability', on which the speaker can momentarily rest while planning the next run. Drilling may help in the storing and retrieving of these chunks as whole units. In this sense, drilling, in effect, is a fluency-enhancing technique. This contrasts with the traditional view that drilling is aimed primarily at developing accuracy.

As a general rule of thumb, drilling involves quick choral (i.e. all the class) repetition of the teacher's model (or a recorded model on tape), followed by individuals randomly nominated by the teacher. It's important that the learners mimic the stress and intonation of the model: there's a world of difference between *How do you SPELL that?* and *How do you spell THAT?*, for example.

For the phrases with 'empty slots', such as sentence starters, the teacher can provide prompts to fill the slot. For example:

| | |
|---|---|
| Teacher: | Do you mind if I sit here? |
| Student 1: | Do you mind if I sit here? |
| Teacher: | smoke |
| Student 2: | Do you mind if I smoke? |
| Teacher: | open the window |
| Student 3: | Do you mind if I open the window? |
| etc. | |

Here, then, are some techniques that involve either individual or choral repetition:

 **Drilling** – the learners are played a recording of an interaction, in which are embedded a number of useful chunk-type items, such as formulaic ways of expressing specific speech acts (as in the dialogue in Chapter 4, page 51). After working on their understanding of the dialogue, they are given the transcript. The recording is played again, but the teacher pauses it at strategic points, and the learners repeat the immediately preceding utterance in unison, and then individually. Only key phrases are repeated, not the whole dialogue. Here, for example, is how part of the above mentioned dialogue might be used:

| Recording | Students |
|---|---|
| **A:** Hey, Barry, what a great tie!<br>**B:** Thanks. Actually, I've had it for ages, but I never wear it. | |
| **A:** It suits you. [pause] | (Chorus) It suits you.<br>(Individual 1) It suits you.<br>(Individual 2) It suits you.<br>(Individual 3) It suits you. |
| Listen, Barry, I was thinking, do you fancy lunch together some time this week? | |
| **B:** That'd be nice. [pause] | (Chorus) That'd be nice.<br>(Individual 1) That'd be nice.<br>(Individual 2) That'd be nice.<br>(Individual 3) That'd be nice. |
| What about Friday?<br>**A:** Perfect. Do you mind if I ask Jackie?<br>**B:** Well, actually, I'm sorry Al, | |

| I'd rather you didn't. [pause] | (Chorus) I'd rather you didn't. (Individual 1) I'd rather you didn't. (Individual 2) I'd rather you didn't. (Individual 3) I'd rather you didn't. |
|---|---|
| etc. | |

As further reinforcement, learners could be asked to underline the drilled segments on the transcript and to mark the main stressed words in each segment. They can then read the dialogues aloud, paying special attention to the underlined sections.

**Chants** – a more playful form of practice that replicates the repeating and chunking nature of drilling is the use of chants. And, because they are contextualized, the chunks in chants may in fact be more memorable than in standard drills. After all, many learners are familiar with catchphrases and idiomatic one-liners from having picked them up listening to pop songs or playing computer games. To work best, the chants should incorporate repeated examples of short, multi-word sequences, and should have a consistent rhythm. It helps if the chants have been prerecorded. Here, for example, is a chant that embeds a number of narrating expressions:

> A funny thing happened …
> *What happened?*
> A funny thing happened to Lee.
> *It's funny how things like that happen.*
> The same thing happened to me.
>
> An awful thing happened …
> *What happened?*
> An awful thing happened to Jim.
> *It's awful how things like that happen.*
> The same thing happened to him.

Having heard it a few times, learners can attempt to reconstruct it in written form, before chanting it in unison. If there is a dialogic element, as in the above chant, the class can be divided in two, each half taking alternate lines. The chanting should be relatively fast, regular, and rhythmic. (Asking learners to mark the main stressed words helps.) Then they can try substituting elements to produce new 'verses', using prompts, such as:

| scary ... Gus ... us | creepy ... Fleur .... her | crazy .... Clem ... them |
|---|---|---|

**Milling activities** – one way of providing repetitive practice of formulaic language in a more communicative framework is to set up a milling activity. This involves learners (space permitting) walking around, asking all the other learners questions with a view to completing a survey or finding a close match. For example, in order to find out how adventurous the class is, each learner first prepares three or four questions that fit this frame:

> Would you ever ... ?

For example, *Would you ever go hang-gliding? Would you ever eat snake?* etc. They then survey the rest of the class, making a note of the number of affirmative answers. This will involve the repeated asking of the question, but in a context that requires re-allocating some attention away from grammatical processing, and on to other mental and physical tasks, such as registering and noting the answers. It is this requirement, the enforced redistribution of attentional resources, that helps the chunking process. According to cognitive skill theory, diverting attention away from a repetitive task forces the streamlining of the separate components of the task into one fluid procedure. Reporting to the class the results of the milling activity (e.g. *Maxim said he would never dive off the high board; Olga said ...*) is also another way of providing repetitive practice where attention is on meaning as much as on form.

Here on the right is a similar sequence from a coursebook, which involves the repetition of formulaic language related to experience and travel:

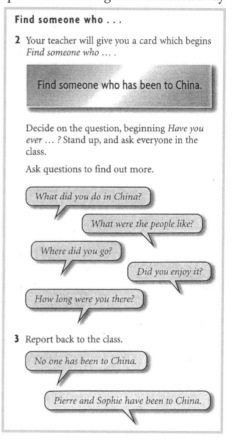

**Find someone who . . .**

**2** Your teacher will give you a card which begins *Find someone who ... .*

> Find someone who has been to China.

Decide on the question, beginning *Have you ever ... ?* Stand up, and ask everyone in the class.

Ask questions to find out more.

> *What did you do in China?*
>
> *What were the people like?*
>
> *Where did you go?*
>
> *Did you enjoy it?*
>
> *How long were you there?*

**3** Report back to the class.

> *No one has been to China.*
>
> *Pierre and Sophie have been to China.*

**Writing tasks**  It may seem strange to have a section on writing in a book that is about speaking. But writing has a useful role to play as an initial stage in the appropriation of newly encountered language for speaking. It can act as a way of easing the transition from learning to using. Inevitably, because of the constraints placed on mental processing by the demands of real-time speaking, learners tend to rely on a very narrow repertoire of memorized expressions in face-to-face interaction. So, an important function of classroom speaking activities is to help learners extend their range of such features. To do this, it may sometimes help to reduce the processing demands placed on them in order to give them time to consciously access alternatives to their habitual repertoire. One way of 'slowing down' processing is to turn the speaking task into a writing one. Here are some ways of doing that:

 **Dictation** – the teacher dictates useful expressions (such as ways of giving advice) and learners write them down, and then compare. Alternatively, the teacher dictates a mixed set of expressions (e.g. ways of giving advice and ways of making requests), and learners write these down while at the same time organizing them into two groups. Or they rank a list of expressions from formal to informal. They then write dialogues, incorporating expressions from the dictated list.

 **Paper conversations** – that is, learners have a 'conversation' with their classmates, but instead of speaking, they write the conversation on a shared sheet of paper. Here, for example, is a paper conversation between two Spanish teenagers:

> Hello, Pablo!
> Hello, Albert!
> What did you do last weekend?
> It isn't your problem.
> Did you see Spain Belgium match?
> I enjoyed.
> Where are you going to Christmas holidays?
> I'm going to go to small village of Soria.
> Which village?
> Molinos de Duero …
>
> [The conversation continues for another 28 lines.]

While the students are writing, the teacher can monitor their written 'conversations' and make corrections or improvements more easily than when students are actually speaking. For example, alongside *It isn't your problem* the teacher first wrote *It isn't your business* before reformulating this as the more idiomatic *It's none of your business*.

 **Computer-mediated chat** – chatting on the Internet by exchanging short typed lines of text is an effective way of 'talking in slow motion'. The talk unfolds in real time, but it is sufficiently slowed down by the need to type so that some attention space is (theoretically) available to focus on improving the quality of the output – by, for example, incorporating some pre-selected discourse features. Researchers, among them Payne and Whitney, have also shown that two hours per week in a chatroom has a significant effect on learners' oral proficiency, compared to learners who don't have this option. See *How to Use the Internet* (Teeler) for ways of setting up chat sessions between students.

 **Rewriting** – asking learners to adapt, improve, or otherwise modify written dialogues is a useful way of practising newly introduced features of speech, such as the use of indirectness, of highly evaluative language, or of more idiomatic language. The dialogue to be adapted can either be provided by the teacher – e.g. written on the board, dictated, or presented on a handout – or it could come from the students' coursebook. It could even have been produced by the learners themselves, by means of the previous 'paper conversation' technique, for example. Learners work together in pairs or small groups to do the editing, one taking the role of 'editor', and the other providing suggestions and consulting dictionaries, if appropriate. The following (invented) dialogue would serve as a good basis for any number of modifications:

> Hello, what's your name?
> My name is Juan.
> What is your nationality?
> I am Venezuelan.
> What is your job?
> I am a student.
> When did you start studying English?
> I started studying English five years ago.
> You speak English very well.
> Thank you, but I would like to improve it.
> etc.

Learners could be asked to make any one or more of the following changes:

- change the register, e.g. to make it more formal, by changing the context, e.g. an airport customs officer interviewing a new arrival.
- make it more interactive, e.g. by incorporating backchannel devices, that is, the listener's comments, such as *Really? Uh-huh* etc, and by distributing the questions between both speakers.
- incorporate more positive appraisal language, e.g. as responses to Juan's answers (*Oh, I love Venezuelan music* etc).
- incorporate performance effects, such as pause fillers and false starts.
- extend the length of the turns.
- incorporate more discourse markers, like *so, well, right, oh*.
- incorporate ellipsis, i.e. leave out redundant language: *What's your name?* [My name is] *Juan*.
- make the talk more idiomatic, e.g. *Where are you from?* instead of *What's your nationality?*, by using phrasal verbs and other idiomatic chunks, as in *I'd like to brush it up a bit* for *I'd like to improve it*. (A good learner's dictionary will help here.)
- make the talk less direct, e.g. by using indirect questions (*Could I ask you … ?*), more modality (*could, might* etc), and vague language (*sort of, kind of*).

Having edited the dialogues, learners can then rehearse them and 'perform' them to the rest of the class.

**Reading aloud**   Just as writing acts as a useful tool for the appropriation of spoken language, so too does reading aloud. In fact, reading aloud is the natural 'next step' between writing and speaking. It is analogous to the way actors read their lines before committing the text of a play to memory. It also has the advantage of providing a secure framework within which learners can focus on lower-level features of talk, such as pronunciation, without the added pressure of always having to plan the next utterance. In this way, reading aloud is a form of scaffolding (see below), but like all scaffolding, it should gradually be dismantled so that learners are finally having to cope on their own without the security of the written text.

Reading aloud fell out of favour at one time because it was felt to be an inauthentic language activity: when, after all, do we have to read aloud in real life? Also, it can be a painful experience listening to someone reading a text aloud that they barely understand. With regard to the first criticism, there are many classroom activities that do not directly reflect real-life language use – dictation being a prime example – but which have well-attested benefits for learners. And the quality of reading aloud can be vastly improved if learners are themselves already familiar with the text: a good argument for having them write the text themselves.

Any of the above writing tasks, therefore, lend themselves to a 'reading aloud' stage. Thus, a dialogue that learners have jointly written can be rehearsed in pairs and then 'performed' to the class. If learners are told that, at some point, they will have to perform the dialogue without recourse to the written text, there will be an incentive both to rehearse it thoroughly and also to commit at least some of it to memory.

But even with a lot of rehearsal, reading aloud can still be a trial for listeners. One reason for this is that readers tend to overlook the importance of the suprasegmental features of pronunciation – stress and intonation in particular – in easing the processing load of listeners. For this reason, it is helpful if learners first mark onto their script the main stressed words and divide each utterance into meaningful chunks.

 In the domain of business English, where giving presentations is a key skill, the writer and educator Mark Powell has developed a useful technique for preparing scripts for reading aloud, which he calls 'sound scripting'. He breaks it down into the following steps:

---

1 Give the learners a short text to 'chunk' – i.e. to decide where pauses would naturally fall, and with what effect. It is not always the case that a long, pauseless run is the most effective in terms of impact. What is important is knowing at what point in a run to pause. Powell argues that pausing after the key content words in a text can be very effective.

2 Learners then highlight the stressed words in each chunk, especially where these serve to mark a contrast.

3 Learners then indicate the sequences of words which could be emphasized by a slower, more deliberate delivery. If they are working on the text on a word processor they can space these words out accordingly.

4 Learners practise delivering the prepared text and then perform the same operations on a text of their choice.

---

Powell comments that 'getting learners to consciously sound-chunk instead of speaking disjointedly takes a little time. They need to get in step with a new rhythm in order to stop themselves getting stranded in the middle of chunks. They need to realize that fluent monologue is not about speaking swiftly but about speaking smoothly in measured phrases. Pausing in the wrong places may frustrate listeners, but pausing in the right places gives the listener time to process the message.' He advises teachers to 'help learners to understand that clear speech and easy listening both rely on effective lexical chunking.'

**Assisted performance and scaffolding**

Sociocultural theory argues that the appropriation of a skill is achieved through the mediation by a 'better other' – what is sometimes called assisted performance.

Assisting performance through scaffolding and other timely interventions is well documented in L2 learning, as in this account of how the writer Edmund White was taught Italian by a private teacher called Lucrezia:

> Her teaching method was clever. She invited me to gossip away in Italian as best I could, discussing what I would ordinarily discuss in English; when stumped for the next expression, I'd pause. She'd then provide the missing word. I'd write it down in a notebook I kept week after week. … Day after day I trekked to Lucrezia's and she tore out the seams of my shoddy, ill fitting Italian and found ways to tailor it to my needs and interests.

This is obviously a useful way of structuring 1-to-1 teaching, but how can such interventions work in a large class? One way is when the teacher builds on the contributions of individuals during open-class (or plenary) talk, such as during the opening chat phase of a lesson or when soliciting opinions about a text that has just been read, or even when answering questions about grammar. In the following extract of classroom talk, the teacher uses a number of devices, such as rephrasing her own as well as the learner's talk in order to provide a secure frame within which the talk can proceed:

> T: … what other advantages do you think you may have, if you were the only child in the family?
> S: I'm sorry? I beg your pardon.
> T: Er, if you were the only child in your family, then what other advantages you may have? What points, what other good points you may have?
> S: It's quieter for my study.
> T: Yes? It's quieter for you to study. Yes? Any other?
> S: No more.
> T: OK. Fine.

A more formalized way of assisting performance is by means of a technique that derives from a teaching method called **Community Language Learning** (CLL). Instead of addressing the teacher directly, the learners sit in a circle and address each other, building up a conversation which, utterance by utterance, is recorded on tape. The teacher's role is to act as a kind of language consultant, providing the language the learners need to express their intended meanings. At beginners' level, this will involve the teacher translating the learners' meanings. At higher levels, it may simply be a question of reformulating what the learner wants to say. Once each utterance has been 'tidied up' in this way, it is committed to tape. Here, for example, is a segment of a conversation that occurred between a small group of adults in a language class in Spain:

| | |
|---|---|
| Student 1: | Emma, where are you going tonight? |
| Student 2: | Tonight I am going to have supper out. |
| Student 3: | Where are you going to have supper? |
| Student 2: | I don't know. I am being taken out. |
| Student 4: | Who are you going with? |
| Student 2: | I am going with – with a guy, but he isn't my boyfriend. |
| Student 1: | And where is your boyfriend? |
| Student 2: | Do you mean now? |
| Student 1: | No, not now. Where will – erm he be this evening? |
| Student 2: | He's going to play water polo. |
| Student 1: | Hmmm, water polo – very interesting! Is your boyfriend hunky? |
| Student 2: | Yes, he is very hunky … |

The above segment lasts less than a minute on tape but took around ten minutes to put together, each line having been tried out and rehearsed before being recorded. Once a sufficient amount of conversation has been recorded, it is played back and transcribed onto the board or an overhead transparency, and it is then available for reading aloud, for some kind of analysis, or for further refinements, such as the addition of discourse markers, backchannel devices (e.g. *really? uh-huh* etc), and so on.

**Dialogues**    Practising dialogues has a long history in language teaching – not surprisingly, since language is essentially dialogic in its use, and any grammar structure or lexical area can be worked into a dialogue with a little ingenuity. Dialogue practice also provides a useful change of focus from teacher-led classroom interaction. Even in large classes with fixed furniture, setting up pairwork is not an insurmountable management challenge.

At this point it is worth distinguishing between the different kinds of paired interaction that are possible. For a start, the dialogue can be enacted by the teacher and a selected student: this is a useful way of demonstrating to the rest of the class how subsequent student–student pairwork is to be performed. For example, the teacher can ask a volunteer student to read aloud one of the roles of a dialogue that appears in the coursebook, while the teacher takes the other role. This is repeated with another student, but this time the roles are reversed. Or the teacher could set up a situation (for example, a hotel reception), take one role herself (e.g. the receptionist), and, with a volunteer student, improvise a dialogue in advance of the rest of the class doing the same in their pairs.

Student–student pairwork can take two forms: open or closed. **Open pairwork** is when two students – either adjacent to, or opposite, one another – perform a dialogue while the rest of the class observes. This is a useful transition phase from the teacher–student stage to the next stage, the closed pairs stage. **Closed pairwork** is when adjacent students perform the dialogue, all pairs working at the same time. The teacher's role at this stage is to move around the class, checking to see that students are 'on task', and offering any guidance or correction, as appropriate. When pairs finish their dialogue, they can be asked to switch roles and do it again, or to change key elements in the dialogue (such as the relationship between the speakers), or to attempt to do the dialogue from memory.

The closed pair stage can be followed by a performance stage, when selected pairs perform the dialogue they have been practising in front of the class. Knowing that this will happen helps 'concentrate their minds' during the closed practice stage and is an incentive to rehearse or even memorize the dialogue. To sum up, a logical sequence of dialogue interactions that moves more and more responsibility onto the learners might be:

1 Teacher takes role A – Student 1 takes role B
2 Student 2 takes role A – Teacher takes role B
3 Student 3 takes role A – Student 4 takes role B (open pairs)
  (repeat as necessary with different students)
4 Students in closed pairs take roles A and B, and then switch roles
5 Selected students enact the dialogue in front of the class

An alternative to stage 3 is to divide the class into two halves, and each half, speaking in unison, takes a role. This works better with younger learners.

Practising and performing dialogues is an effective way of providing conditions for the appropriation of newly encountered language features. A balance needs to be found, however, between security and challenge. Making the task too easy, as when students are given unlimited time to simply read a dialogue aloud, is unlikely to motivate them to make the kind of adjustments in the current state of their knowledge that are needed in order to integrate new knowledge. On the other hand, placing too much performance pressure on learners too soon may have the effect that they fall back on their existing competence, avoiding the risk-taking that is necessary if their competence is to be extended. One way to ease pressure on learners is to give them sufficient time to rehearse before asking them to perform in front of the class. Another is not to place too high a load on their ability to remember the dialogue. Here are some ways of easing the memory demands of dialogue practice, while at the same time providing optimal conditions for the incorporation of new language items:

 **Items on board** – having isolated, from a taped dialogue, and drilled a number of expressions (e.g. such communication strategy formulas as *how do you say … ? It's one of those things that …* etc), the teacher writes these on the board and leaves them there as learners attempt a speaking activity (such as buying items in a department store). As the learners incorporate these expressions into their talk, the items are successively rubbed off the board.

 **Chunks on cards** – learners work in pairs to have a dialogue, and each has a set of cards with useful expressions on them, such as *by the way*, *speaking of which* etc. The idea is to include as many of these features into the conversation as naturally as possible as it develops, adding the card to a discard pile each time it is used. This can be turned into a game – the first person to discard all their cards is the winner.

A variation of this idea is called Discussion bingo:

## Discussion bingo

**1**  You are going to play a game of bingo. Follow the rules below.

**BINGO** *rules*

Work in groups of three. Each of you has one of the bingo cards below. Choose a topic from the box or choose one of your own and start a discussion. As you are speaking you must try to use all the expressions on your bingo card. Each time you use one cross it off. When you have used all of the expressions on your card, shout 'Bingo!' As long as the other group members are happy that you used the expressions correctly, you are the winner.

| taste | learning English | good food | city life | personality |
| identity | art | luck | the 21st century | |

**CARD 1**

Talking of …
It seems that …
When I was younger, I'd often …
Not necessarily, because …
I really regret …
Oh, come on …

**CARD 2**

Frankly, …
Gone are the times …
I really do wish …
There is no doubt that …
People will always …
Only when …

**CARD 3**

Actually, …
It's not known whether …
If only …
You must bear in mind …
I tend to …
On the whole …

**2**  Choose a different card and a different topic and play again.

 **Memorizing scripts** – as we saw in Chapter 2, many speech events follow fairly predictable paths. Typically, interactants in transactional encounters – such as obtaining service in a shop, ticket office, restaurant, or lost property office – follow certain shared scripts: a greeting and its response, an offer to provide service, a request etc. Learners can prepare for these kinds of encounters by learning the script (and any plausible variations). One way of doing this is first to ask them to order a jumbled dialogue. For example:

Yes, it's first on the right, after the lights.
Yes?
Thanks very much.
Excuse me?
You're welcome.
Can you tell me where Hills Road is, please?

Alternatively, they first hear the dialogue on tape in its entirety, and then line by line, repeat after the tape. Useful 'chunks' (e.g. *You're welcome*) can be drilled more thoroughly. Learners then practise the dialogue in pairs until they can do it from memory. They can also practise variants of the dialogue, substituting different items into key 'slots', e.g. *It's second on the left, after the bridge.* The dialogue can be further adapted, to take account of changes in the situation – e.g. an informal dialogue can be made formal by changing the relationship between the speakers, or a face-to-face dialogue could be turned into a phone dialogue.

The extract on page 76 from a beginners' coursebook exploits the predictable structure of three 'service encounter' scripts.

 **Picture and word cues** – to ease the memorizing load, the script of the dialogue can be represented on the board either in the form of drawings or word prompts, such as *Hills Road?*, *right – lights* etc. The drawings need not be very sophisticated – they are simply there as a memory aid. As the learners become more proficient at the dialogue, the prompts can be erased one by one.

 **Flow-diagram conversations** – this is similar to the previous idea, but involves representing a dialogue in terms of its speech acts (or functions). Learners, in pairs, perform the dialogue, following a route through the different functions, selecting from memory appropriate expressions for the different speech acts. Here is an example flow diagram:

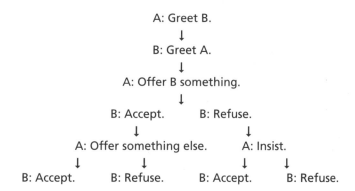

A: Greet B.
↓
B: Greet A.
↓
A: Offer B something.
↓
B: Accept.        B: Refuse.
↓                    ↓
A: Offer something else.        A: Insist.
↓            ↓            ↓            ↓
B: Accept.    B: Refuse.    B: Accept.    B: Refuse.

Alternatively, the learners can listen to a recording of a dialogue and choose the flow diagram that matches it, as in the coursebook sequence on page 77.

 **Conversational 'tennis'** – this is a technique for encouraging a greater degree of interactivity in student–student talk. The teacher uses an example dialogue on a recording to isolate and highlight the following three conversational features:

- that it's conversationally helpful to provide two pieces of information for every one question asked, e.g. A: *What did you do yesterday?* B: *I worked all day. Then I went to the gym.*

# 10 Things people buy

## 1 At the market

1 Look at the market stall. What can you see?

2 Here are three conversations. Put them in the right order.

| | | |
|---|---|---|
| Yes, here you are. | I'll have one, please. | It's size 38. |
| £25. | Here you are. That's £1. | Hello. Can I help you? |
| How much is it? | Blue, I think. | Yes. What size is that jacket? |
| All right, 20 then. | How much are these lighters? | Oh, that's too big. Thanks anyway. |
| Oh no, that's too expensive. | What colour do you want? | |
| 1  Can I see that radio? | They're £1 each. | |

⌨ Now listen and check your answers.

3 Choose some other things on the market stall. What questions can you ask about them?

Can I see … ?   How much … ?   What size … ?   … ?

4 Role-play

*Student A*: You work at the market stall. Sell things to B.
*Student B*: You're a customer. Buy things from A.

• **Everyday English.**

**Invitations**

1 Listen to three dialogues inviting friends out. Which follows which pattern below?

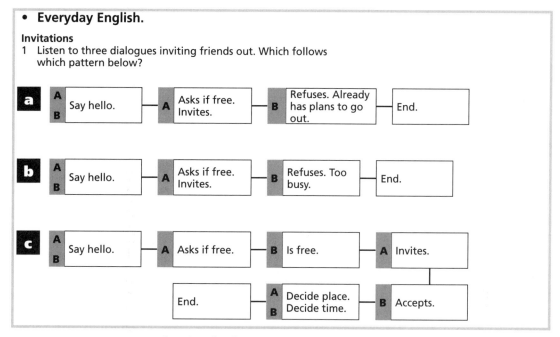

• that involved conversationalists respond to answers with a show of interest: e.g. B: *Did you? Really? Wow!* etc.
• that it's helpful to return a question with another question, e.g.:
   **A:** *What did you do yesterday?*
   **B:** *I worked all day. Then I went to the gym.*
   **A:** *Did you?*
   **B:** *What did you do?*

Once these features have been highlighted and practised in isolation, set the learners the task of having a conversation in which they try to follow these rules as much as possible, batting the conversational 'ball' back and forth as much as possible, without letting it drop. Repeat this activity regularly, e.g. as a regular warm-up stage at the beginning of every lesson.

 **Disappearing dialogue** – the text of a dialogue is written on the board (or is projected using an overhead projector). Learners practise reading it aloud in pairs (either open or closed), and then the teacher starts removing sections of it. Initially these sections may simply be  individual words, but then whole lines can be removed. By the end of the activity, the dialogue has 'moved' from the board into the learners' memories. They can then be challenged to write it out from memory.

 **Dialogue building** – this is similar to the script memorizing ideas above, except that the dialogue is not presented to the learners but is elicited from them, line by line, using visual and verbal prompts. The stages of the process of building a dialogue are the following:

1 Establish the situation, using drawings of (usually two) stick figures on the board.

Ask questions to elicit the situation based on visual clues in the picture, e.g. 'Where are they?' 'Who are they?' 'Do they know each other?'

2 Having established a context and a purpose for the exchange, e.g. 'the man wants a room for the night', the teacher starts to elicit, line by line, the conversation. Depending on the level of the students, as well as the predictability of the dialogue, it can be prepared in advance, so that the teacher has a clear idea of how the dialogue will develop. Or it can simply be constructed organically, on the basis of what the students come up with. A hotel reception dialogue is one which – in most cultural contexts – follows a fairly predetermined script, and therefore should not require a lot of pre-scripting on the part of the teacher. A dialogue between two friends meeting by chance in the street, on the other hand, may require some pre-scripting, since there are so many possible conversational outcomes, once the initial greetings have been dealt with. The exact combination of preparation and spontaneity will depend, in the end, on the teacher's experience and teaching style.

3 The teacher starts by eliciting the first line of the dialogue. In the hotel reception scenario, it might be the receptionist saying, 'Good morning. Can I help you?' This is drilled a few times, both chorally and individually, the teacher correcting where necessary and insisting on natural sounding rhythm and intonation. It helps if students are familiar with the question 'Where's the stress?' It is also important that, for drilling purposes, the lines of the dialogue are short, e.g. not more than about eight to ten words. Anything longer may need to be segmented, preferably into tone groups.

4 The teacher then elicits ideas for the second line of the dialogue, i.e. how the guest responds. The teacher shapes and corrects the class's suggestions, until an acceptable response has been achieved, e.g. *Yes, I'd like a room for the night*.

5 Now, the two lines are put together. (This is why the technique is called 'dialogue *building*'.) Using the interactional framework

*[Handwritten annotations in left margin: "good idea ✳" and "First say it in your native language then translate it?"]*

outlined above, the teacher and an individual student practise the two-line exchange before it is 'handed over' to the class in open and closed pairs.

6   This process continues until the complete dialogue has been built up, each line 'laid down' and drilled, with frequent recappings of the whole dialogue, using picture or word prompts on the board as memory aids. Of course, the whole process need not be quite so elaborate, especially if only a few lines are in play. Nor should the dialogue be too long, or the learners' patience, as well as their memory load, may be overstretched.

7   Finally, two students are chosen to perform the dialogue in front of the class. Variations to the original script can be introduced – by changing the details of the guest's needs, for example (these can be written on role-cards). Or the teacher could introduce a 'blocking' element (see below) in order to encourage spontaneity and creativity.

8   Now the dialogue can be elicited back from the students and written on to the board so that learners have a copy to take away.

## Communicative tasks

Fundamental to the view that speaking is a cognitive skill is the idea that knowledge becomes increasingly automated through successive practice. Practice makes – if not perfect – at least, fluent. A corollary to this view is that the automating process can be speeded up by creating practice conditions that 'park the attention'. That is, the kind of practice that helps automization is best when the learner's attention is distracted from the temptation to refer to the rules of grammar and to generate every utterance from scratch. If learners are given unlimited time to dwell on the rules, it is unlikely that there will be any push to 'chunk' these rules to cope with the demands of real-time processing. It is only by driving in traffic, after all, that novice drivers are compelled to automate the processes of changing gear, indicating, checking the rear-view mirror etc. If they were to devote all their attention to these actions, they would be at risk of ignoring what's happening on the road.

One way to distract attention from a dependence on declarative knowledge is to increase the processing demands of the task, such as reducing the time available, as we will see on page 84 in the discussion on task repetition. Another way is to set a task that requires attention to be directed at achieving some extralinguistic goal, such as buying a bus ticket or winning an argument. We saw this at work in the milling activities, described earlier. The communicative demands of the task discourage learners from dwelling on the facts of the language, and compel them, instead, to draw on automated routines. Communicative tasks, thus, fulfil two important language learning needs: they prepare learners for real-life language use, and they encourage the automization of language knowledge.

Communicative activities are characterized by the following features:

* the motivation of the activity is to achieve some outcome, using language;
* the activity takes place in real time;

- achieving the outcome requires the participants to interact, i.e. to listen as well as speak;
- because of the spontaneous and jointly constructed nature of the interaction, the outcome is not 100% predictable;
- there is no restriction on the language used.

A classic communicative task type is the **information gap activity**. In information gap activities, the information required to complete the task is distributed amongst the interactants. There is a knowledge gap, therefore, between them, and this can only be bridged by using language. So, in order to achieve the task outcome, the interactants have to communicate. Here, for example, is an information gap activity from a coursebook:

Here is a transcript of two elementary Spanish-speaking learners doing this task:

> **A:** Er, near, near, near this man, who play the violin, there is a, a dog?
> **E:** No (No) I don't have a go … , a dog in my picture.
> **A:** A dog near, OK. Mm. The, the motorbike is, er, is, um, near in, in, in the bottom of the … you, you are a, a bike of the bottom of the picture?
> **E:** In the bottom?
> **A:** Yeah.
> **E:** Mm … no.

Continues …

> **A:** No?
> **E:** In my picture, the bike is …
> **A:** Near the man of …
> **E:** Near of …
> **A:** Near one man he stay, er, with, with a pen, in a, in a table.　　[*He said he couldn't remember 'writing'.*]
> **E:** Bicycle, or motor …
> **A:** A motor, motorbike.
> **E:** Yes, is near.
> **A:** Is near, in the bottom of the, of the, of the picture. The bottom, bottom.
> **E:** Yes. Um, sorry, do you have a one man, er, in he hand a flowers?
> **A:** No, it haven't.
> **E:** Is a two difference for me (OK) I think. Um …

The task continued for some time until all the differences had been identified, generating a good deal of output on the part of both learners, and some fluent, if inaccurate, runs.

More elaborate information gap activities, involving several participants, are sometimes called jigsaw activities. Here is an example of a four-party jigsaw activity:

 **Jigsaw activity** – prior to the lesson, the teacher prepares four flashcards, each an enlarged frame from the following picture story.

The teacher tells the class they are going to witness a minor traffic accident, but, as in most traffic accidents, it happens very quickly, and they only see the accident from one perspective. The class is divided into four groups and the teacher flashes the pictures, in random order and for a few seconds only, one per group. The members of each group have to then agree, amongst themselves, what it is they have just seen. (This stage is also useful for checking vocabulary.) Then, the members of each group are redistributed, so that new groups are formed that comprise someone from each of the original four groups. (One way of doing this is to give each member of each group a number: 1, 2, 3, and so on. Then all the 'number ones' form a group, and all the 'number twos', and so on.) The task of each group is (a) to take it in turns to describe what each person saw; (b) to decide, jointly, the sequence of the accident; and (c) to decide, as a group, who was to blame.

To do the task, learners will be compelled to fulfil the conditions of a communicative activity outlined above. And, as in real life, there will always be some difference of opinion as to what exactly happened. Where there is difference of opinion and the built-in need to resolve that difference, learners will be compelled to use language in such a way that they will be distracted from a concern for formal accuracy.

Another way of distracting the attention is to incorporate a competitive or game-type element into the task, whereby groups are competing with each other to achieve an outcome ahead of the others. Here is one such activity:

 **Info-gap race** – the teacher pre-teaches or revises nouns relating to geometrical shapes, such as *line*, *square*, *circle*, *triangle*, and *rectangle*, as well as prepositional phrases such as *on the left*, *on the right*, *above ...*, *below ...*, *outside ...*, *inside ...*, so that learners can describe a design such as the following.

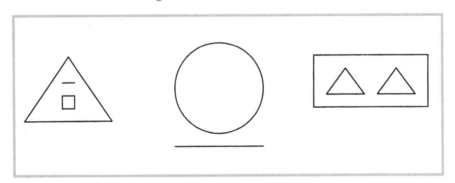

To practise, the teacher 'dictates' a design – that is, describes it so that the learners can draw it correctly. For example, *On the left there is a triangle. Inside the triangle there is a small square and above the square there is a straight line ... .* The learners do the same to each other in pairs.

Now the game element is introduced. The class is divided into two teams, and the blackboard is divided in two by a line down the middle. Each team has a representative at the board, each with a piece of chalk, or boardmarker. In advance of the game, the teacher should have prepared a dozen or so different designs incorporating the geometrical shapes, large enough to be seen by all the class. The teacher ensures that the two team representatives at the board can't see the designs, and then selects one and shows it to the two teams. Each team attempts to describe the design to its representative at the board, and the first team to do this successfully, so that the design is replicated on the board, is the winner of that round. The teacher then selects another design and the game continues.

The game can also be played with simple pictures of, for example, landscapes or room interiors.

Here are some more communicative speaking task types that help promote automatic processing, and hence develop fluency:

 **Surveys** – these are simply more elaborated versions of the milling activity described earlier, and involve learners asking and answering questions in order to complete a questionnaire or survey, based on a topic that the teacher has suggested, or which occurs in the coursebook. For example, the learners may be asked to prove or disprove the claim that men take after their fathers and women take after their mothers. The idea is that learners prepare – in pairs or small groups – survey-type questions, such as *Is (or Was) your father interested in football? Are you?* etc, and then mill around, asking the questions, noting the answers, before returning to their original groups to collate their results. A spokesperson from each group then reports the groups' findings to the class, whereupon the class decides, as a group, whether the claim is justified or not.

A class survey forms the basis of this lesson sequence from an intermediate coursebook:

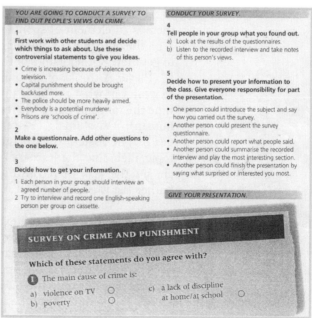

**Blocking games** – many of the dialogues that learners practise follow a fairly predictable route, for example, an exchange encounter at a railway station ticket office, ordering a meal in a restaurant, or a dialogue in which someone is phoning a business to ask to speak to one of its staff. Learners typically listen to, read, rehearse, and then perform these dialogues, to the point that they hardly have to listen to what their classmate is saying any more. In order to introduce an element of unpredictability into such dialogues, one of the speakers (typically the one providing a service) can be encouraged to 'block' the other one's expectations. The teacher can demonstrate by asking one of the students to take a role – for example, the customer's role in a shopping situation which has been thoroughly practised. The teacher takes the role of the shop assistant. Instead of providing the expected response (e.g. *Yes, certainly. What size do you take?* in answer to the request: *I'd like to buy a pair of trainers.*) the teacher says *I'm sorry, I'm new here. What are trainers?* or *Have you tried our sports department?* or *Trainers? Don't you mean gym shoes?* The 'customer' then has to cope with this unexpected response, and any others that the 'shop assistant' comes up with subsequently. Students can then play the 'blocking game' in pairs themselves, exchanging roles and partners from time to time. The element of unpredictability means that learners have to 'park their attention', drawing on their language survival skills to get their meanings across.

 **Guessing games** – finally, a number of guessing games, such as 'What's my line?', in which one learner thinks of a job and the others have to ask *yes/no* questions to guess what it is, provide ideal conditions for automating knowledge: they are inherently repetitive (*Do you work indoors or outdoors? Do you work with your hands? Do you wear a uniform?* etc); there is two-way interaction (players have to listen to the answers to the questions they have asked); the game takes place in real time, so there is an element of spontaneity and unpredictability; and the focus is on the outcome (i.e. winning the game) not the language being used to get there. Other games of this type include: 'What sort of animal am I?' (Player A thinks of an animal; Player B has to ask *yes/no* questions to work out what the animal is); 'Animal, vegetable, or mineral?' (this time the range of guessable items is extended to almost anything non-human); 'Who am I?' (Player A thinks of a famous person, alive or dead). The basic format of such games can be applied to almost any topic, including the learners' own lives. For example, in pairs, learners are set the task of reconstructing their partner's weekend activities (either last weekend or next weekend) by asking only *yes/no* questions.

**Task repetition**   In Chapter 2 we listed the contextual factors that make speaking easy or difficult, and which therefore have a knock-on effect in terms of fluency. Cognitive, affective, and performance-specific factors were identified. For L2 speakers, the same factors apply, but their effect can be even more marked, affecting not only the fluency but the accuracy and complexity of the learner's production. With the advent of task-based learning, researchers have been interested in discovering how these factors impact on task design and task outcomes. By manipulating the conditions of speaking tasks, they have found, for instance, that:

- giving learners unlimited time when performing a task increases their accuracy, but at the expense of their fluency;
- allowing time for pre-task planning enhances fluency, and this is manifested in a faster speech rate and fewer silent pauses;
- likewise, pre-task planning has a positive effect on the complexity of the language that is produced, as manifested by more complex syntax and lexis – about ten minutes' planning time seems to be optimal;
- however, the effects on accuracy of pre-task planning are less convincing – it seems to depend on the grammar area in question, as well as the kind of task, and the disposition of the learner;
- moreover, planning time does not seem to increase the amount of formulaic (chunk) language learners use;
- individual planning shows better outcomes than teacher-led planning, or group planning;
- interactive tasks produce more accuracy and complexity, but monologic tasks produce greater fluency;
- if the task outcome requires learners to make justifications, more complex language will result;
- repeating a task shows gains in accuracy (including pronunciation), fluency, and complexity, but these gains don't necessarily transfer to other, similar tasks.

By calibrating, then, factors of planning, interactivity, outcomes, and task repetition, teachers can influence the outcome of tasks. Repeating a task shows the most consistent and wide-ranging gains over all, although the jury is still out as to the extent that these short-term gains translate into long-term ones. That is, we still don't know whether appropriation results, leading to long-term improvement. However, as we saw in Chapter 1, 'abnormally fluent' speakers, such as race-callers and auctioneers, get constant practice at the same kind of 'task', suggesting that task familiarity, if not exact repetition, is a factor in the development of fluency.

On page 86 there is an instance of task repetition from Gairns and Redman, in which three students (two Japanese and a Taiwanese) recount a narrative based on a picture story. Their first and third attempts at the tasks are juxtaposed.

Apart from the greater concision and precision of the third account, what is interesting is how individuals 'borrow' elements that other students previously introduced. So, in the third attempt, T recycles the sentence *They are/were fed up* that both N and J had originally used. This suggests that task repetition may provide opportunities for appropriation, especially of formulaic and idiomatic language.

Simply repeating a task, however, is unlikely to be hugely motivating for learners unless there is some obvious incentive to do so. In the case of the narrative on page 86, the learners were keen to 'get it right', perhaps because they knew they were being recorded. This suggests that recording learners doing a task is one way of getting them to repeat it, but with an extra element of challenge. Also, knowing that they are going to be recorded may have the useful 'washback effect' of making them work harder during the rehearsal phase.

| First attempt | Third attempt |
| --- | --- |
| J: They went to the park by car and he go with his dog and he take lunch box and I have sandwich and hamburgers.<br><br>T: champagne …<br><br>J: champagne, sandwich and very peaceful but later many people will come, will came, … many people came here and one people played football and the dog is barking there …<br><br>N: They were fed up … a man listening to music …<br><br>J: And a child shout very loudly, shout very loud … they are fed up and they decide to go home.<br><br>T: They went to car park … they looked to a man, hold a brick …<br><br>J: They see … they saw one people hold a brick and they will smash his car's window and they feel very scared … and the dog barked … and the man very scared.<br><br>N: The man screamed, shouted … Tom, maybe he was surprised and his dog bite, bit this guy.<br><br>J: The man fight with … the man with the brick … and this man didn't stole, didn't steal anything.<br><br>T: This man couldn't run away … and the woman call the police and the police will come, will came and arrest them. | T: It was a nice sunny day so Tom and Victoria decided to go to picnic in the countryside. They went to picnic by car with their dogs, his name is Jim. They had lunch box and champagne, sandwiches and hamburgers.<br><br>N: They found a nice place near the lake … very peaceful.<br><br>J: Felt relaxed, but later one family come and the man was playing football, the girl singing, the dog was barking and the man listen loud music.<br><br>T: They were fed up. They decided to go home. They went to the car park, er … a man hold a brick and smashed the window.<br><br>J: The man will … the dog bit the man and the man shouted …<br><br>T: Tom shouted, 'That's my car. What are you doing?'<br><br>N: Tom and this man had … fighting, had a fight, then Jim bit the man and they couldn't go, run away, and the woman called the police, and the police came and arrest, arrested them. |

Here are some other ways of providing learners with an incentive to repeat a speaking task:

**The Onion** – if the number of students in the class is not more than about twelve, they can be divided into two equal groups. As many chairs as there are students are arranged in the centre of the classroom in two circles, the outer circle facing the inner circle. The students sit opposite one another and perform their speaking task – it might, for example, involve telling their partner about a current worry that they have and getting advice. The students in the outer circle then move round one chair so that they have a new partner, and the activity is repeated until all the pairs in the 'onion' have interacted. At the end, they can then report to the group on the advice they received – which was the most helpful, unusual, impractical etc?

**The Poster Carousel** – this is similar to 'the Onion', in that half the students move while the other half remain in the same spot, and at each move the speaking task is repeated. This time, however, the activity is done standing. To start with, the learners, working individually or in pairs or in groups of three, prepare a poster on a pre-selected theme. It may, for example, represent a particular hobby or leisure interest, or it may illustrate aspects of their job, or their biography, or their family, or a trip they have recently been on. Or it may be based on a text they have read. For example, if the class has an ESP (English for Special Purposes) focus, they could each be given a different article or academic paper to read, which they then reproduce in the form of a poster. Half the students then stand by their posters while the others circulate, moving from poster to poster, asking questions about each one, with a view to getting as clear as possible an idea of its content. Once all the presenters have been 'interviewed', the roles are reversed, and those who have been asking the questions then stand by their own posters and become the interviewees. This activity is good practice for students who may in fact be preparing to attend conferences where this kind of poster presentation occurs. But it is also an excellent way of building repetition into a speaking task. To encourage learners to engage with the task, the teacher can set an objective, such as deciding on the most interesting presentation, or writing a summary of the similarities and differences between different presentations.

**Headlines** and **Art Gallery** – these are variations of the 'Poster Carousel' idea, except that, in the case of Headlines, each student prepares a 'headline' that summarizes a newsworthy event in their recent lives (such as *Frustrating Shopping Trip* or *Interesting New Restaurant Experience*). Half the students stand with their headlines written on sheets of paper, and answer the questions addressed to them by their classmates in order to reconstruct the 'story' behind the headline. Then the roles are reversed. In the case of 'Art Gallery', the posters of 'Poster Carousel' are replaced by postcards of paintings (or even the students' own original 'art works') that individuals have to explain to those who are milling around asking questions. At the end of the activity, students can vote on what they thought was the most convincing explanation.

**4-3-2** – in this pairwork format, the objective is to retell a story or monologue within a time limit that decreases at each retelling, thereby encouraging greater automaticity. Students are paired and take it in turns to do a monologic speaking task, e.g. recounting a story or explaining a process, based on picture prompts, or summarizing a text they have each read. For the first 'telling' each speaker is allowed four minutes (the listener can be responsible for timing the speaker). The second time round they have to achieve the same degree of detail but in only three minutes, and the task can be repeated a third time, but in two minutes. (The timings can vary according to the nature of the task and the degree of challenge that is desirable. 4-2-1, for example, may be more appropriate for more fluent speakers.)

**Conclusions**  In this chapter we have looked at ways that learners may achieve greater control over their own speaking through classroom processes of *appropriation*. Activities aimed at appropriation provide learners with a supportive framework in which they can *practise control*. The support may take the form of:
- a model, which is repeated, as in drills or chants.
- a writing task, which allows longer processing time than does 'live' speaking.
- reading aloud from a text.
- the teacher's scaffolding of the learner's talk by, for example, reformulating or translating learner utterances.
- memorized, and rehearsed, dialogues.
- repeating a task, e.g. by doing it with different interactants.

The support needs to be gradually reduced so as to encourage a degree of independence, which in turn will require a degree of appropriation. This support reduction may take the form of, for example:
- removing the model, so that learners have to rely on memory.
- withdrawing teacher support.
- moving from the written mode to the spoken one.
- reducing planning time.
- performing the task under more exacting conditions, e.g. to a time limit, or in public.

**Looking ahead**  We have now looked at two of the stages of our three-stage model of skills development: awareness and appropriation. It is time therefore to consider the third and final stage: autonomy. In the chapter that follows we will review ways that learners can experience and achieve greater autonomy in speaking, including the capacity for self-development, self-monitoring, and unassisted performance.

# 6 Towards autonomy

- Autonomy and automaticity
- Criteria for speaking tasks
- Feedback and correction
- Presentations and talks
- Stories, jokes, and anecdotes
- Drama, role-play, and simulation
- Discussions and debates
- Conversation and chat
- Outside-class speaking

**Autonomy and automaticity**

In the diary he kept of his Portuguese-learning experience in Brazil, the researcher Dick Schmidt records the frustration of being a beginner:

> Week 2
> I *hate* the feeling of being unable to talk to people around me. I'm used to chatting with people all day long, and I don't like this silence. … Today P and I were at the beach, a guy came up for a cigarette, sat down and wanted to talk. He asked if I were American, and I said *sim*. He said something I didn't comprehend at all, so I didn't respond. He said, 'Well, obviously communication with you would be very difficult' (I *did* understand that, though I can't remember any of the words now), and left.

Three months later, Schmidt was able to report:

> Week 18
> Last night I was really up, self-confident, feeling fluent … At one point, M said to F that she should speak more slowly for me, but I said no, please don't, I don't need it anymore.

In no longer needing others to assist him, Schmidt had achieved a degree of **autonomy** that was a far remove from his initial helplessness. This autonomy (which applied only in certain situations: he confessed that he still couldn't have fielded questions in Portuguese at the end of a lecture) was partly due to the increased **automaticity** of his language production, what he experienced as 'feeling fluent'. As we have seen, the ability to automatize the more mechanical elements of a task so as to free attention for higher-level activities is one characteristic of skilled performers, whether the skill be driving a car, playing a musical instrument, or speaking a second language. Other characteristics of skilled performers are:

- **speed** – skilled performers work fast, although speed alone is not the only indicator of skilfulness
- **economy** – skilled performers ignore inessentials and know how to carry out tasks using minimal means
- **accuracy** – skilled performers are quick at detecting and rejecting errors
- **anticipation** – skilled performers can think and plan ahead
- **reliability** – compared to unskilled performers, skilled performers are less likely to under-perform in adverse conditions

In sociocultural terms, autonomy is the capacity to self-regulate performance as a consequence of gaining control over skills that were formerly other-regulated. Moreover, the self-confidence gained in achieving a degree of autonomy, however fleeting, can be a powerful incentive for taking further risks in this direction. This is why classroom speaking activities that involve minimal assistance, and where learners can take risks and boost their confidence, provide an important launch pad for subsequent real-world language use. This is particularly the case if the classroom learner is performing under what are called **real operating conditions**, i.e. those conditions that involve the kinds of urgency, unpredictability, and spontaneity that often characterize real-life speech events. It is one thing, for example, to deliver fluidly a prepared speech, but it is quite another to respond to questions from the audience at the end. In this chapter we will look at ways that learners can experience a degree of autonomy as speakers and in real operating conditions. This will first involve establishing some general criteria for selecting and designing classroom speaking tasks as well as a discussion on how best to provide feedback, including correction, on such tasks.

**Criteria for speaking tasks**

In order to maximize speaking opportunities and increase the chances that learners will experience autonomous language use, the following conditions need to be met:

- **Productivity** – a speaking activity needs to be maximally language productive in order to provide the best conditions for autonomous language use. If students can do an information gap task by simply exchanging isolated words, or if only a couple of students participate in a group discussion, the tasks may hardly justify the time spent setting them up. This is also the case, of course, if learners are speaking mainly in their L1.

- **Purposefulness** – often language productivity can be increased by making sure that the speaking activity has a clear outcome, especially one which requires learners to work together to achieve a common purpose. For example, the aim of having to reach a jointly agreed decision can give a discussion more point and encourage the participation of all members. Requiring learners to report to the class on their discussion is also an effective way of ensuring a greater degree of commitment to the task. A competitive element – such as turning the task into a race – can also help.

- **Interactivity** – activities should require learners to take into account the effect they are having on their audience. If not, they can hardly be said to be good preparation for real-life language use. Even formal, monologic speaking tasks such as talks and presentations should be performed in situations where there is at least the possibility of interaction, e.g. where there is an audience present, one which can demonstrate interest, understanding, and even ask questions or make comments at the end.

- **Challenge** – the task should stretch the learners so that they are forced to draw on their available communicative resources to achieve the outcome. This will help them experience the sense of achievement, even excitement, that is part of autonomous language use. Of course, if the degree of challenge is *too* high, this can be counterproductive, inhibiting learners or reducing them to speaking in their L1. The teacher needs to be sensitive to the degree of difficulty a task presents individual learners and to adjust the task accordingly.

- **Safety** – while learners should be challenged, they also need to feel confident that, when meeting those challenges and attempting autonomous language use, they can do so without too much risk. The classroom should provide the right conditions for experimentation, including a supportive classroom dynamic and a non-judgmental attitude to error on the part of the teacher. Also, learners need to be secure in the knowledge that the teacher – like a driving instructor – will always be there to take over if things get seriously out of hand.

- **Authenticity** – speaking tasks should have some relation to real-life language use. If not, they are poor preparation for autonomy. Of course, many classroom activities – such as drills and language games – can be justified on the grounds that they serve the needs of awareness-raising or of appropriation. But, in order to become autonomous, learners will need to experience a quality of communication in the classroom that is essentially the same as communication outside the classroom. This means that they will, at times, need to perform in real operating conditions, e.g. spontaneously, unassisted, with minimal preparation, and making do with their existing resources. It also means that the kinds of topics, genres, and situations that are selected for speaking tasks bear some relation to the learners' perceived needs and interests.

**Feedback and correction**

It is often a delicate decision as to how to provide learners with feedback on their errors when their attention is primarily focused on the content of what they are saying, rather than on the way they are saying it. Interrupting learners 'in full flight' to give them corrections seems to run counter to the need to let them experience autonomy. If the teacher is constantly intervening to assist their performance, whether by providing unknown words or correcting their errors, they can hardly be said to be self-regulating. And it may have the counterproductive effect of inhibiting fluency by forcing learners' attention on to accuracy.

Nevertheless, many teachers feel uncomfortable about 'letting errors go', even in fluency activities, and there is support for the view that maintaining a **focus on form** – that is, on formal accuracy – is good for learners in the long run. It is important, therefore, that such a focus should be effected at minimal cost to the speaker's sense of being in control. In the following extract, the teacher's corrections, while explicit, are unobtrusive, and these are picked up by the learners with no real loss of fluency:

| Learner 1: | And what did you do last weekend? |
| Learner 2: | On Saturday I went on my own to Canterbury, so I took a bus and I met [Learner 6] – he took the same bus to Canterbury. And in Canterbury I visited the Cathedral and all the streets near the Cathedral and I tried to find a pub where you don't see – where you don't see many tourists. And I find one |
| Teacher: | Found |
| Learner 2: | I found one where I spoke with two English women and we spoke about life in Canterbury or things and after I came back |
| Teacher: | Afterwards |
| Learner 2: | Afterwards I came back by bus too. And on Sunday what did you do? |
| Learner 1: | Oh, er, I stayed in home |
| Teacher: | At home |
| Learner 1: | On Sunday I stayed at home and watched the Wimbledon Final … |

In the above extract, the teacher's interventions are economical and effective, and the conversational flow is not threatened. However, it could be argued that such overt monitoring deprives the learners of opportunities to take more responsibility for their own monitoring and self-repair. This is especially the case with regard to their mistakes, as opposed to their errors. By **mistake** is meant the learners' momentary failure to apply what they already know, due mainly to the demands of online processing. An **error**, on the other hand, represents a gap in the speaker's knowledge of the system. Mistakes can usually be self-corrected, but errors cannot. A deft hint to the learner that they have used a present verb form instead of a past one, for example, may be all that is needed to encourage self-correction. And self-correction, even if prompted by the teacher, is one step nearer self-regulation and the ultimate goal of full autonomy.

Sometimes, however, the learner's message is simply unintelligible, and some kind of more obtrusive intervention is necessary to repair the breakdown. In this case, an intervention that is perceived by the learner as **repair** is likely to be less inhibiting than one that is perceived of as correction. Repair is facilitative, while correction can be construed negatively, as judgmental. For example, in this extract, the teacher's intervention takes the form of a conversational repair, one that is consistent with the meaning-orientation of the interaction:

| | |
|---|---|
| Learner: | ... so I phone the doctor and ask for a *consulta* ... |
| Teacher: | I'm sorry? A what? |
| Learner: | I ask for a, er, for see the doctor. |
| Teacher: | An appointment? |
| Learner: | Yes, ask for appointment |

If it is the learners themselves who are interacting, it may be the case that the other learners can initiate the repair. This is more likely if the design of the task is such that mutual understanding is necessary if the task outcome is to be achieved. In a describe-and-draw task, for example, where one learner describes a picture to another, who has to reproduce it, a breakdown in communication should normally force some kind of repair process. Otherwise the task would never be completed. It is important, therefore, that learners are equipped with the language with which to initiate repair, such as *Sorry, could you say that again? I didn't get that* and *What do you mean, X?* Many teachers ensure these expressions are available to students by having them permanently displayed as posters on the classroom wall.

An alternative to on-the-spot correction is to postpone it until the end of the activity. This means that the teacher needs to keep a record of errors while the speaking activity is in progress. These can either be given to individual learners as 'feedback notes', or dealt with orally in open class. In either case, it is generally more motivating if the learner's successes as well as their failures are recorded. One way of doing this is in the form of a feedback sheet, as in this example:

| Name: Teresa | |
|---|---|
| Task: Telling an anecdote | |
| Things I liked: | Points to note: |
| 1 The bar was completely empty ... <br> 2 description of the woman <br> 3 use of past continuous: 'the bag was hanging on the chair ...'; 'You thought I was trying to ...' (but see 3 opposite) | 1 sitting at a table (not 'on') <br> 2 no one apart from us (not 'of') <br> 3 we didn't pay attention (not 'take'), and better in continuous: 'we weren't paying attention' <br> 4 she sit □ she sat <br> 5 she get up □ she got up <br> 6 to steal your wallet (not 'rob') <br> 7 how can you think this of me (not 'from') |
| General comments: You established the situation and characters well, and used direct speech to dramatic effect. Watch irregular verbs in past! (sat, get etc). Also use 'said', not 'told', with direct speech: she said 'You thought I was ...' etc. | |

Alternatively, recording learners on audio or video provides a useful record of their speech for subsequent analysis and improvement. As we saw in Chapter 4 (page 60), asking learners to make their own transcriptions of these recordings and to suggest ways of improving them yields positive results, both in terms of what they notice and also in terms of subsequent performances.

**Presentations and talks**

Whether or not learners will have to give presentations or talks in 'real life', the experience of standing up in front of their colleagues and speaking for a sustained turn is excellent preparation for real-life speaking. This is especially the case if they also have to respond to questions from the floor. The following ideas belong to this category of speech event:

 **Show-and-tell** – asking learners to talk and answer questions about an object or image of special significance to them works well for all age groups and at all but the most elementary levels. Show-and-tell can be established as a regular feature of lessons, with learners taking turns and knowing in advance when their turn is due. The talk itself need be no more than two or three minutes, and unscripted, although the use of notes can be permitted. Extra time should be allowed for asking questions. Suggestions for topic areas can include such things as hobbies, sports, holidays, family, and work, but the focus should be on a specific object or image. For students who are unfamiliar with this format, it is a good idea if the teacher models a show-and-tell herself.

 **Did you read about …?** – this is a variant of 'show-and-tell' and can be done in small groups rather than to the whole class. The stimulus is 'something I read in the paper or heard on the news' rather than an object. If all learners know that this is an obligatory lesson starter, they are more likely to come prepared. In groups, they take turns to relate their news item to the rest of the group. The most interesting story in each group can then be told to the class as a whole.

 **Academic presentations** – students who are studying English for academic purposes are likely to need preparation in giving academic presentations or conference papers. In advance of practising these skills in class, it may help to discuss the formal features of such genres as well as identifying specific language exponents associated with each stage. (Having an example presentation on videotape or audiotape would, of course, be extremely useful.) A checklist of features, along with useful expressions, can be displayed as a poster in the classroom, and this can be modified over time as students take turns giving their presentations and discussing their effectiveness. For example, a group of mixed native speaker and non-native speaker graduate students in Canada, who each had to give an oral academic presentation (OAP) about a research paper they had read, came up with the following key features of such presentations:

- The OAP should contain a concise summary, a thoughtful and well-balanced critique, and a list of relevant implications.
- Presenters should engage and evoke interest in the audience.
- Presenters should have an effective delivery style.
- Presenters should manage time well.

 **Business presentations** – the same principle, that of peer presentations in conjunction with collaborative analysis and critical feedback, works effectively with business presentations as well. One way of reducing the pressure of solo performance is to ask learners to work in pairs on the preparation of the presentation and to take turns in its delivery. It is important to allow a question-and-answer session at the end since this is invariably the most challenging stage of a presentation. The 'audience' should be given a little time at the end of the presentation to prepare their questions. This in turn could be followed by some discussion as to the strengths and weaknesses of the presentation. Alternatively, the presenters can be asked to reflect on, and evaluate, their own performance. The following checklist is a good example of how an evaluation could be structured. It comes as part of a sequence in which students practise the introduction stage of a presentation:

---

If possible record yourself. When you play back your introduction, use the checklist below to help you evaluate your presentation.

| Checklist | Yes / No | Example phrases |
|---|---|---|
| ■ Did you explain to the audience:<br> – Who you are?<br> – Why you are speaking? | | |
| ■ Did you include a statement of purpose? | | |
| ■ Did you include signposting? | | |
| ■ Did you relate the presentation to the needs of the audience? | | |
| ■ How did you involve the audience? | | |
| ■ Did your opening remarks include:<br> – a participatory activity?<br> – a question to the audience?<br> – surprising / unusual facts? | | |

---

One problem with student presentations is the question of how to maintain audience interest. Setting the other students some kind of task is one way round this. A checklist, like the example above, could also serve equally well as a listening task. Alternatively, the other students could be set the task of coming up with at least three questions to ask, or of taking notes with a view to making a short summary of the presentation.

**Stories, jokes, and anecdotes**

Storytelling is a universal function of language and one of the main ingredients of casual conversation. (Remember the kedgeree story in Chapter 1?) Through their stories learners not only practise an essential skill, but they can also get to know one another: we are our stories. The neurologist Oliver Sacks, in *The Man Who Mistook His Wife for a Hat*, writes:

---

Each of us is a singular narrative, which is constructed continually, unconsciously by, through, and in us – through our perceptions, our feelings, our thoughts, our actions; and, not least, our discourse, our spoken narrations. Biologically, we are not so different from each other; historically, as narratives – we are each of us unique.

---

Narration has always been one of the main means of practising speaking in the classroom, although this used to take the form of having learners recount folk tales, or amusing or dramatic incidents based on a series of pictures. More recently, the value of encouraging learners to tell their own stories has been recognized, and coursebooks now include personalized narrating tasks, whether monologic or dialogic, as a matter of course. Two are shown on page 97 (1 and 2).

Other ideas for storytelling-based activities are:

 **Guess the lie** – learners tell each other three short personal anecdotes, two of which are true in every particular, and the third of which is totally untrue (but plausible!). The listeners have to guess the lie – and give reasons for their guesses. They can be allowed to ask a limited number of questions after the story. It helps if the teacher models this activity in advance of the learners doing it.

A variant of this idea is to guess who a story originated from. Page 97 (3) shows how the idea is developed in a coursebook:

 **Insert the word** – learners are each given a card with an unusual word or expression – perhaps one that has come up recently in class – which they keep secret. They then take turns telling each other an anecdote in which they incorporate their 'secret item' as unobtrusively as possible. At the end of each telling, the others have to guess what the word or expression was.

 **Chain story** – in groups, the learners take turns to tell a story, each one taking over from, and building on, the contribution of their classmates, at a given signal from the teacher.

 **Party jokes** – learners first each learn and rehearse a joke that has a narrative element. They then simulate a party, standing up and milling, and exchanging jokes in pairs or groups of three. They should first be taught some basic joke-framing expressions, such as *Did you hear the joke about ...?* and *That reminds me of the joke about ....* . The repeated practice that they get telling their jokes fulfils an important function of good speaking tasks. At the end of the activity the class can vote on the best joke.

**Drama, role-play, and simulation**

Speaking activities involving a drama element, in which learners take an imaginative leap out of the confines of the classroom, provide a useful springboard for real-life language use. Situations that learners are likely to encounter when using English in the real world can be simulated, and a greater range of registers can be practised than are normally available in classroom talk. For example, situations involving interactions with total strangers or requiring such face-threatening speech acts as complaining and refusing, can be simulated with relatively low risk. Formal language that would not normally occur in the classroom context can be practised. Moreover, simulation and artifice suit the temperament of certain learners, who may feel uncomfortable 'being themselves' in a second language. On the other hand, there are also learners who feel self-conscious performing in

**Anecdote**

**1**

Think about a lucky or an unlucky experience you have had. You are going to tell your partner about it. Choose from the list below the things you want to talk about. Think about what you will say and what language you will need.

☐ Was it a lucky or unlucky experience?
☐ When did it happen?
☐ Where were you?
☐ Who were you with?

☐ What were you doing?
☐ What happened?
☐ Why was it lucky (or unlucky)?
☐ How did you feel afterwards?

**2**

## 4 MAKING CONVERSATION

### The first time

In pairs, **A** choose two 'first times'. Tell **B** about what happened. **B** listen and ask for more information. Swap roles.

**A** *I'm going to tell you about the first time I drove a car. I was staying in the country with my uncle and he had an old Renault 4…*
**B** *How old were you?*

**The first time I…**

bought a record or CD
went to a live concert
smoked a cigarette
fell in love
travelled by plane
went abroad
drove a car
saw a lot of snow
earned some money
had to go to hospital

*last group*

**3**

### 🔊 prepare your story

5 **Think!** You're going to tell a partner about a good or bad shopping experience. Read the checklist.

**checklist**
– Use the questions in the framework to help organize your story.
– Use a dictionary or ask your teacher to help you with new words.
– Make notes, but don't write the full story.
– When you've finished, practise telling the story to yourself. This will help your confidence.

### 🔊 tell your story

6 Work with a partner. Tell each other your stories. At the end, make sure you understand each other's stories. Use the phrases in the **natural English** box if necessary.

**asking for clarification**

I didn't understand the bit about …
Could you explain the bit about … again?
I'm sorry but I didn't understand what / why / when / how …

7 You're now going to tell your partner's story. Tell it as if it's your <u>own</u> story. You may need to make small changes to sound realistic. Your partner should correct any factual mistakes you make.

8 Work with a <u>new</u> partner. Tell the two stories, without saying which one is yours. Your new partner can ask you questions. At the end, they have to decide which was your story, and why.

front of their peers, especially if this involves a degree of improvisation, and care has to be exercised in choosing and setting up such activities so as not to make even more demands on them than speaking in another language normally requires. Just as in the real theatre, a preparation stage, including rehearsal, is generally recommended in advance of public performance.

A distinction can be made between role-plays and simulations. The former involve the adoption of another 'persona', as when students pretend to be an employer interviewing a job applicant or celebrities mingling at a party. Information about their roles can be supplied in the form of individualized role-cards. For example:

| Father | Mother | Son |
|---|---|---|
| You are an ex-hippie and have brought up your son (now 18) according to your progressive, left-wing values. | You often have to mediate between your husband and your 18-year-old son. | You have decided to join the army, and you are now going to tell your parents. |

In a simulation, on the other hand, students 'play' themselves in a simulated situation: they might be stuck in a lift or phoning to arrange an outing, for example. A more elaborate simulation might involve the joint planning and presentation of a business plan. Drama is the more general term, encompassing both role-play and simulation, as well as other types of activities, such as play-reading, recitation, and improvisation.

What follows is a selection of drama activity types, chosen because they are potentially highly language productive, can be adapted to different levels of proficiency and for different topics, and because they allow learners to experience autonomy in the speaking skill. They also have the added advantage of requiring few or no materials, and hence can be set up spontaneously and in most teaching contexts:

 **Alibis** – this classic activity has a game element, in that the participants have to try and outwit each other, and can be played several times with no loss of interest. The basic format starts with two students being 'accused' of having committed some crime, such as a robbery in the institution where the class takes place, in a fixed period, say between the hours of 10 and 11 in the morning on the preceding day. The two 'accused' then have to establish an alibi, and they go out of the room to do this. The alibi needs to account for their actions only during the time period in question (anything before or after is irrelevant), and it is important to establish that they were together for all that time. While the accused contrive their alibi, the rest of the class can prepare generic questions, with the teacher prompting, if necessary, of the type: *What were you doing …? What did you do next? Did you meet anyone? What did you say? How much did it cost? Who paid?* etc. The accused are then led in, one at a time, and have to answer the questions put to them. (It helps to establish the rule that they are not allowed to claim that they don't remember.) Any significant discrepancy in their answers means that they are, of course, guilty.

With large classes, the activity can also be done in groups, each group playing their own version of the game. Alternatively (and so long as they are out of earshot), the two accused can be interviewed simultaneously by two different groups, and then exchange places.

A variant is 'Green Card', in which immigration officers interview, separately, two candidates who claim to be members of the same family (in which case, they have to answer questions about the other members of their immediate family – their name, age, and appearance) or who claim to be partners (in which case, they have to answer questions about their daily routine). Here is a coursebook version of the same idea.

---

**Get talking**

**9  In groups of 4, roleplay an immigration interview.**

Students A and B: Turn to page 86.
Students C and D: Turn to page 89.

**Lesson 38, Exercise 9, Students A and B**

**1  You are a married couple.**
B is from another country. Immigration officers are going to interview you and you have five minutes to prepare for the interview. Work together to make sure you give the same information about:
- how long B has been in the country
- how long you've known each other
- where you met
- your wedding
- your jobs
- what you do in your free time

**2  Student A: Answer Student C's questions.**
**Student B: Answer Student D's questions.**

**3  Discuss your interviews. Do you think you gave the same answers?**

**Lesson 38, Exercise 9, Students C and D**

**1  You are immigration officers.**
A and B are married. B is from another country and you don't think it's a real marriage. You are going to interview the couple and you have five minutes to prepare for the interview. Work together to prepare questions to ask them. You will ask both A and B the same questions, about:
- how long B has been in the country
- how long they've known each other
- where they met
- their wedding
- their jobs
- what they do in their free time

**2  Student C: Ask Student A your questions.**
**Student D: Ask Student B your questions.**

**3  Compare A and B's answers. Are they telling the truth?**

Another variant of 'Alibis' is 'UFO', in which two people are interviewed separately about an alleged encounter with aliens.

 **Shopping around** – this role-play has an inbuilt repetitive element, and is a variant of the 'carousel' idea (see page 87), in which pairs of students visit every 'shop' before making a decision as to which one to patronize. The class is divided into two: one half are the customers and the other are the providers. These are further subdivided into pairs. The situation itself can vary to suit whatever theme is appropriate. For example, the customers might be parents looking for a particular kind of school for their special needs child; the providers represent different schools. In their pairs, the parents first decide what features the school they are looking for should have. Meanwhile, also working in pairs, the schools each devise a policy, with regard to such things as discipline, the curriculum, uniforms, sports, and so on. (It is important, however, that the school fees are the same for each school: the mere cost shouldn't be a deciding factor.) When everyone is ready, each set of parents interviews one of the schools. They then move round one, and interview the next school, and so on, until all the parent pairs have interviewed all the school pairs. The parents are then ready to make their decision as to which school they prefer, while the schools can decide which parents they prefer. Each group reports their decision – and the reasons – to the class.

Variants include: choosing a package holiday; choosing a language course; choosing flatmates; choosing a wedding venue; and so on. A version of this basic format can also be used to role-play job interviews, as in this example:

---

### Job interviews

**1** Which of the following suggestions about conducting a job interview do you agree with? Add some of your own.

a) There should be more than one interviewer.
b) The interviewer should sit behind a desk.
c) The interviewer should make notes while the interviewee is speaking.

**2** In groups of four, choose one of these advertisements and discuss the points for and against the job.

**ADMINISTRATOR**

Administrator with experience and word processing skills required to work in our friendly but busy school office. An interest in Shiatsu and Natural Health an advantage. Please send full CV to: The British School of Shiatsu, 188 Old Street, London EC1 9BP.

**GOLDEN SKI HOLIDAYS**

seeks mature person to run chalet holiday programme in Alps. Outgoing personality and ability to work hard without supervision essential. Good cooking and housekeeping skills an advantage. Modest salary but accommodation and meals provided and abundant skiing time. Apply giving full details to: Golden Ski Holidays Ltd, 2 Ridge Street, Aldershot, Hants.

**NURSERY NURSE**

Experienced, qualified person required to fill vacancy for full-time nursery nurse. Duties include special responsibility for two-and-a-half-to-four-year-olds at private nursery. 40 hour working week. Apply in writing to: The Principal, Phoenix Nursery, Pond Lane, Guildford, Surrey GU1 3DD.

Each of you is a candidate for the job your group has chosen. Decide on:
– your qualifications (e.g. university degree, specialised training).
– your experience (e.g. with computers, a similar organisation, children).
– your qualities (e.g. enthusiasm, patience, administrative skill).

**3** The interview panel will consist of the three people in the group not being interviewed.

a) Arrange the chairs.
b) Take turns to be interviewed. The candidates should sound interested and enthusiastic. The interviewers should try to find out the candidates' strengths and weaknesses.
c) Vote for who you think should get the job.

**The Inquiry** – an inquiry has been set up to gather evidence and opinions about some miscarriage of justice or consumer complaint. Different interest groups are represented, and they put their case to a team of independent investigators in an open forum. The situation might be a disastrous package holiday, a housing estate that is plagued with problems, a badly governed village, and so on. After the situation has been established, the different interest groups brainstorm their problems, while those responsible try to anticipate these and muster counterarguments. The panel of arbitrators – two or three students – prepares questions to ask the complainants. Each interest group then puts its case, and time is allowed for the groups to counter each other's arguments. Finally, the arbitrators make a ruling.

Variant: the same format can be used for 'The Tender', in which different interest groups submit their proposals for a project. The project might be the development of an open space in the middle of a town, or how best to provide energy for a village, or the design of a commemorative stamp or monument, for example. 'The Heart' is another variation, in which representatives of patients needing life-saving surgery make their case: profiles of each candidate will need to be prepared.

 **The Soap** – learners plan, rehearse, and perform (and, if possible film) an episode from a soap opera. The soap opera could be based on a well-known local version, or on a selection of magazine pictures of people who become the 'characters'. The advantage of using the soap opera format is that learners can draw on a shared stock of melodramatic situations but are not compelled to come up with a clever ending. And, of course, they can continue the story by inventing subsequent episodes.

With regard to this last idea, Charlyn Wessels, an EFL teacher in Scotland, describes how she structures a whole term's work around drama techniques, culminating in the production of a full-length play based on the class's improvisations. One such play was a soap opera, generated by the learners themselves through brainstorming activities. Here, for example, is the 'relationship tree' the class developed for the plot of the soap opera:

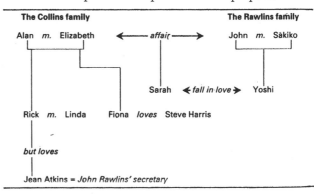

*Figure 2: One group's relationship tree for Soap Opera*

101

Students write detailed profiles of the characters they are going to play, and then the story is built up through a series of improvisations and scripted. Work is done on pronunciation as well as using drama techniques to improve performance. After the final performance one student commented, 'I've improved my English, had fun, and I've got to know my friends much better – what more can I ask of a course?'

**Discussions and debates**

Many teachers would agree that the best discussions in class are those that arise spontaneously, either because of something personal that a learner reports or because a topic or a text in the coursebook triggers some debate. Here, for example, a teacher describes how one such discussion erupted in a class of Catalan teenagers:

> I was trying to get attention at the beginning of the class but two of the girls were so deeply engrossed in a conversation in Catalan that it was proving even more difficult than usual. Finally, I said to these two girls that if their conversation was really that interesting they should tell the rest of the students, in English, what they were talking about. One of the girls proceeded to tell the class about a girl at her school who was wreaking havoc by telling lies about people and generally being very destructive. The rest of the students listened with good attention, then asked questions, made suggestions, and the conversation developed for the next twenty minutes or so.

In this case, the teacher knew how to take advantage of the students' concerns, and turn this into a discussion activity in English. In the absence of such opportunities, however, it is useful to have a store of techniques for setting up discussions in a more formal way. Here are some generic discussion formats.

 **Discussion cards** – the teacher prepares in advance sets of cards (one for each group) on which are written statements relating to a pre-selected topic. In their groups, one student takes the first card, reads it aloud, and they then discuss it for as long as they need, before taking the next card, and so on. If a particular statement doesn't interest them, they can move on to the next one. The object is not necessarily to discuss all the statements: the teacher should decide at what point to end the activity. Groups who have finished early can prepare a summary of the main points that have come up. These summaries can be used to open up the discussion to the whole class. The topic may, for example, be fashion, and the statements to discuss might include the following:

> Fashion is universal.
> Fashion is an art form.
> People should not be judged by what they wear.
> Fashion is simply a way of making people spend money.
> Fashion celebrates diversity.
> The fashion industry is unethical.
> etc.

Alternatively, the discussion points could be phrased as questions, with a view to eliciting a more personal response, such as:

> How important is the label on an item of clothing?
> How often do you shop for clothes?
> Would you wear – or have you worn – second-hand clothes?
> How would you describe your style of dress?
> etc.

There is, of course, no reason why the learners shouldn't be able to prepare the cards themselves, especially they are about a topic they have experience in or have been reading about. Groups then prepare a set of cards and exchange them with other groups.

 **Warm-up discussions** – when introducing a new topic or preparing learners to read or listen to a text, it is common to set a few questions for pair or group discussion, followed by a report back to the whole class. These discussion questions may target general knowledge about the topic (in which case they could be set as a homework research task) or some personalized response to the topic. Here, for example, is a warm-up discussion task that introduces a coursebook unit on sport:

# On the ball

## Speaking

Discuss these questions.

1  Which is your favourite sport? Why do you like it?
2  Do you play it, watch it or both?
3  What sports do you dislike? Why?
4  Which sports do you associate more with men or women? Why?

*My favourite sport is squash. I love it because it's really fast – afterwards you feel great!*

 **Balloon debate** – this popular format is based on the idea that a hot-air balloon with its cargo of passengers is dangerously overloaded and at least one of the passengers has to be jettisoned. The group members, representing famous people in history, famous living people, or people in different professions, put their case as to why they should be saved and why someone else should be sacrificed. This works best if students have had time to prepare their case, and this can be done in pairs. For example, if there are enough students to form two 'balloons', matched pairs from each balloon first work together, before re-forming in order to stage the debate.

**Pyramid (or Consensus) debate** – the principle of this format is that at first individuals work in pairs to achieve consensus on an issue, and then these pairs try to convince other pairs, before forming groups of four, and so on, until the whole class comes to an agreement. For example, the teacher might set the class the task of devising some 'class rules' with regard to such things as classroom etiquette, discipline, duties, homework etc. First, individuals draft a list of a maximum of, say, eight rules. They then compare in pairs, and draft a new list of eight rules, that they are both agreed on. This will normally involve some discussion and negotiation. Once they have their list, they join forces with another pair, and the process begins again. Finally, the two halves of the class come together to agree on the definitive version.

Other ideas that work well in this format are ranking tasks – e.g. the five most important people in history; the ten best pop songs of all time; the eight things I would take to a desert island; the six school subjects that should be compulsory, and so on. Or students take a bare statement and qualify it in such a way as to make it acceptable. For example:

> Children should be beaten.
> Smoking should be banned.
> Anyone should be allowed to adopt children.

The same principle – of reaching some kind of consensus – can be used with more imaginary situations, such as the following:

---

**A party for all time**

Work in groups:
You can hold a party for eight guests from today or history.

- Which eight people will you invite and why?
- Who will be the 'guest of honour'? i.e. The most important guest?
- What will the seating arrangement at the dinner table be?
- What will the menu be?
- You can ask ONE guest ONE very important or personal question only. Who would you ask, and what would your question be?

---

 **Panel discussions** – these adopt the format of a television debate in which people representing various shades of opinion on a topic – such as some locally relevant issue – argue the case, usually under the guidance of a chairperson. One way of organizing this is to let students first work in pairs to marshal their arguments, then one of each pair takes their place on the panel, while the others form the audience – who can, of course, ask questions once the panellists have stated their point of view. It helps if the classroom furniture is organized to represent a real panel discussion. It also works better if learners are allowed to choose their point of view themselves, rather than having to voice an opinion they may not be party to. However, some sensitive topics work best if the activity is set up as a role-play (see above) and participants are given clearly defined roles (e.g. police officer, psychiatrist, single parent, social worker etc). They can then 'hide behind' these roles. In large classes, the panel discussions can take place concurrently in groups, with the teacher monitoring between them.

As a final comment, discussions will work much better if learners are equipped with a repertoire of expressions for voicing strong agreement, strong disagreement, and all the shades of opinion in between. These could be available on posters around the room and regularly reviewed and topped up. Some useful expressions include:

| Expressing an opinion:<br>*If you ask me, …*<br>*(Personally), I think …*<br>*If you want my opinion, …* | Conceding an argument:<br>*Perhaps you're right.*<br>*OK, you win.*<br>*You've convinced me.* |
|---|---|
| Strong agreement:<br>*Absolutely.*<br>*I couldn't agree more.*<br>*I totally agree.*<br>*I agree.* | Hedging:<br>*I take your point, but …*<br>*Yes, but …* |
| Qualified agreement:<br>*That's partly true.*<br>*On the whole, yes.*<br>*I'd go along with that.* | Strong disagreement:<br>*I don't agree.*<br>*On the contrary …*<br>*I totally disagree.* |

**Conversation and chat**

Attitudes to classroom conversation and casual chat have varied over the years. In the heyday of audiolingualism, one writer, Louis Alexander, warned that 'the traditional "conversation lesson" is of no value at all if the student is not ready for it … . The student must first be trained to use patterns in carefully graded aural/oral drills. Only in this way will he finally learn to speak.' The chat stage of the lesson, if it occurred at all, was simply there as a curtain raiser to the main event – the controlled practice of sentence patterns. Until recently, one London language school was still advising its students that 'the teacher and the student must not chat during the lesson. They must only ask and answer the questions in the book. Chatting is a waste of time.'

Such a view sits uncomfortably with the finding that conversation, i.e. casual talk that is primarily interpersonal (see page 13), is by far the most common and the most widespread function of speaking. Moreover, there is a school of thought that argues that, in L1 acquisition, the development of conversational skills precedes the development of language itself. As Evelyn Hatch put it, 'language learning evolves *out of* learning how to carry on conversations', i.e. out of learning how to communicate. By extension, it has been argued that conversation in a second language is not the *result* of language learning, but it is the site where learning occurs.

It is also, of course, a fact that many language learners feel that their most urgent need is to develop conversational competence, and they regularly choose 'conversation' as their principal objective when answering needs analysis surveys. For this reason, many language schools offer 'conversation classes' as a way of complementing more traditional, grammar-focused, classes. However, these offer a challenge to teachers and course designers since it is difficult to plan or programme something as inherently unstructured and spontaneous as casual conversation. As one writer puts it, 'genuine conversational interactions cannot be the outcome of planned lesson agendas, they have to *emerge* – and so, by definition, cannot be planned.'

One way that teachers get round this is to organize conversation classes around a set of themes. Ideally, these should be negotiated with the learners in advance, through the use of a questionnaire or by means of a consensus debate, as outlined in the section above. Theme-related texts can be used to trigger conversation, either in open class or in groups. Or individual students take turns to make a short presentation on the pre-selected topic, which is then followed by open discussion. Pre-planned lesson content can take the form of teaching useful conversational formulas and routines, such as how to open and close conversations, how to interrupt, change the subject, ask for clarification, and so on. Or the focus could be on the teaching of communication strategies, such as paraphrasing, using vague language, and pause-fillers (see page 29).

Alternatively, conversation 'lessons' can be incorporated into normal classwork. One teacher in the USA, Gisela Ernst, describes how she does this through the use of what she calls **talking circles**:

> The talking circle is a total group activity that generally takes place at the beginning of the 45-min conversational English class. Almost every day, teacher and students gather in the talking circle to share and discuss experiences, anecdotes, news, special events, introduce the weekly theme, and the like. Although the teacher might open the discussion by suggesting a general topic, the overriding assumption is that the talking circle provides a place and an audience for students to discuss anything of interest to them.

This assumes, of course, that the classroom dynamic is such that learners are prepared to 'share and discuss experiences'. In order to create the right conditions for such exchanges, it often pays to start with more structured activities which incorporate an element of personalization. Here are three such activities:

 **Sentence star** – the learners each draw a five-pointed star on a piece of paper. The teacher asks them to write on the tip of the first point *can*, on the second point *like*, on the third point *have*, on the fourth point *used to*, and on the fifth point *going to*. (These prompts can of course be varied according to the level of the class, the syllabus etc.) Individually, they then write true sentences about themselves using each of the five words on their star, following the teacher's example, e.g. *I can speak a little Portuguese*. In pairs or small groups, they take turns to read each other their sentences. The others in the group have to ask at least five questions about each of the sentences (e.g. *Where did you learn Portuguese? How well can you speak it? Can you write it?* etc). In a final, open-class stage, people can report on interesting things they have learned about their classmates.

**True/false sentences** – the teacher dictates about five or more sentences to the class. If desired, at least some of the sentences can embed a specific grammar structure, although this is not necessary. For example:

> Every summer I go somewhere different.
> Last year I went to Peru.
> I have never been to Brazil.
> I haven't been to Colombia, either.
> I'd like to go to Guatemala.
> etc.

The teacher tells the class that some of the sentences are true and some are false. They work in pairs to try and guess which are which and then report their guesses, with reasons. Then, working individually, and using the dictated sentences as a model, they write some true and false sentences about themselves and take turns to guess which sentences are true or false in pairs or small groups.

 **One of us/Some of us** – the teacher writes the following sentence starters on the board:

> One of us can …
> Two of us can …
> Three of us can …
> All of us can …
> None of us can …

(Again, the grammar structure embedded in these prompts can be adapted.) The learners are organized into groups of four and asked to generate as many true sentences about their group as possible in, say, ten minutes, using the above sentence starters. A spokesperson from each group reports some of the group's sentences, and these can be used as the basis for an open-class question-and-answer stage. For example:

> Spokesperson: One of us can play the guitar.
> Teacher: Oh really, let me guess who that could be? Ernesto, is it you … ?
> etc.

The above activities can help break the classroom ice, but little or no conversation will be possible in the classroom unless the teachers can demonstrate their willingness to be conversational partners, too. This will mean, at times, relinquishing their traditional pedagogic role in order simply to talk to the learners.

As was argued in Chapter 2, traditional IRF exchanges may 'cramp' the learners' conversational style. At times, therefore, it may be useful if teachers hand over at least some of the question asking to the learners. Here, for instance, is a short extract from a lesson where the teacher is simply engaging with her teenage ESL learners conversationally:

| | |
|---|---|
| Teacher: | You watched the *Hero and the* ... where, and the where? |
| Keiko: | Weirdo. |
| Teacher: | And the weirdo ... *Hero and the Weirdo* ... I've never heard of that movie ... . Is it scary? |
| Keiko: | Yeah, scary ... . You like? |
| Teacher: | Tan? Did you want to say something? Is there a movie that you like? |
| Tan: | Scary movie. |
| Teacher: | You like scary movies? I think everyone likes scary movies. |
| Keiko: | Oh, you like? |
| Teacher: | No, I don't like them, but, I can only watch a couple, I get nightmares, I'm a baby. |
| Keiko: | I know, I know, when you saw them, you scared when you sleep and then you scared they coming and they beat you up. |
| Teacher: | That's right, that's right ... Sometimes I get scared after watching a scary movie ... I have nightmares. |

Finally, many teachers have discovered the benefits of bringing guests into the classroom in order to talk with learners. Apart from providing a new focus of interest, a guest can expose learners to a different accent and vocal style and, especially if the guest is not a teacher, can provide experience interacting in ways that more naturally reflect real-life communication. A simple technique that works well is to ask learners to prepare a few questions in advance. They then 'interview' the guest as a class, allowing the guest's answers to fuel further questions. They can then write up a summary of the interview in pairs or small groups.

**Outside-class speaking**

Real autonomy is only achievable if learners can cope on their own in the real world. To ease the transition from the classroom to the outside world, there are a number of things they can do outside the class. For example:

**Tape diaries** – learners keep a taped diary by recording themselves regularly at home on audiotape and submitting this to the teacher for feedback. One teacher describes how he set this activity up:

> Once a week, with certain exceptions, students were to make an entry in their journals by recording themselves speaking in English for about three minutes ... The content of the recordings could cover observations on topical events and issues, discussion of ideas and information received, or consideration of any matters related to study or daily life. Students were advised to minimize hesitation by organizing their ideas before approaching the recorder. After the entries were submitted to me, I recorded my responses and returned the tapes.

This technique appears to suit some learners who may be timid about speaking in class, judging by this extract from one of the taped journals:

> Last time when we talked about *Dead Poets Society*, I didn't have the courage to speak out in class. Here I would like to share with you my opinions about the movie ...

Moreover, preparing the journals allowed some of the learners to experience autonomous language use, as this extract attests:

> These days, because I have to make up several of my journal, I kept thinking about what to say and how to say it in English and then I record my journals again and again. All day long, I am thinking in English and speaking English. It seems that I am in the United States again.

If learners have access to voice mail, the recordings can be exchanged digitally, as email attachments, saving a great deal of time and inconvenience. All that is required (apart from online access) is a microphone and speakers, and an email program that supports voice mail. This also allows the teacher to send written comments in the accompanying email. Comments need not be exhaustive: it's probably enough to respond to the content of the recording (*That bit about your homestay family was interesting ...*) and make a couple of suggestions.

 **Audio and video conferencing** – these are virtual meetings, in which two or more people communicate via a live audio or video link over the Internet. They require microphone, speakers, and special software, as well as fast and reliable Internet access, and, in the case of video conferencing, a web camera. Both audio and video conferencing have been used to good effect to bring learners from different parts of the world together to collaborate on tasks and simulations. As the technology improves and costs come down, such electronic means offer enormous potential in terms of out-of-class speaking practice.

 **Human–computer interaction** – while this may still seem in the realm of science fiction, computer programs have already been devised that, by responding to written input, simulate human–human interaction. These are called **chatterbots**. Here, for example, is a 'conversation' I had with a web-based chatterbot:

> Coco: Hi Scott.
> Scott: Hi Coco.
> Coco: How are you today Scott?
> Scott: Fine, and you?
> Coco: Aside from pms, I'm doing fine.
> Scott: What's pms?
> Coco: Aside from pms, I'm doing fine.

Continues ...

> Scott:  Let's change the subject. I'm writing a book about speaking.
> Coco:  You go ahead and change the topic. Have you checked the library for information?
> Scott:  On speaking?
> Coco:  I understand most of it but sometimes it becomes difficult because we can't tell what expression should be felt when speaking to each other.
> Scott:  Do you mean pragmatics?
> Coco:  Well, no, I do not mean pragmatics.

Although some chatterbots are able to synthesize speech, sustained conversation is still some way off, given the current state of automatic **speech recognition** software and the enormous amount of data that would have to be inputted. However, where the context is tightly constrained, so that the number of possible utterances is limited, it is now possible for some degree of human–computer spoken interaction to take place. At least one such program, for the practising of elementary Japanese, already exists. As more and more language educators and publishers embrace computer technology, and as the technology itself develops, it is quite likely that a certain amount of interactive speaking practice using computers will soon be a reality.

 **Portfolios and diaries** – asking learners to reflect on their out-of-class speaking experiences is a useful way of raising their awareness as to their strengths and weaknesses and also of monitoring their progress over time. Moreover, by sharing these experiences with other learners they may be motivated to try out strategies that seem to have worked for their colleagues. And, of course, talking about language use is another way of practising speaking. One way of sustaining this reflection process is for learners to keep a journal or portfolio of their extracurricular language use. Here, for example, is an extract from the journal of a Czech woman, Martina, who has emigrated to Canada, in which she recalls her difficulties speaking on the phone:

> The first time I was very nervous and afraid to talk on the phone. When the phone rang, everybody in my family was busy, and my daughter had to answer it. After ESL course when we moved and our landlords tried to persuade me that we have to pay for whole year, I got upset and I talked with him on the phone over one hour and I didn't think about the tenses rules. I had known that I couldn't give up. My children were very surprised when they heard me.

The idea of learners keeping a 'language biography' as part of a larger portfolio of language-learning achievements is an essential feature of the European Language Portfolio, and its purpose is described on the Council of Europe website:

> The Language Biography facilitates the learner's involvement in planning, reflecting upon and assessing his or her learning process and progress; it encourages the learner to state what he/she can do in each language and to include information on linguistic and cultural experiences gained in and outside formal educational contexts; it is organised to promote plurilingualism, i.e. the development of competencies in a number of languages.

The 'language biography' idea can be integrated into classroom activities in a less formal way, by simply asking learners to share their experiences of out-of-class language encounters. The teacher's own stories – of embarrassments and successes using a second language – can provide a useful model. They can also act as an indirect form of learner training – a way of feeding in suggestions as to how to maximize speaking opportunities outside the classroom. Personal stories of the kind 'When I was living in Peru, I organized a conversation exchange with one of my neighbours ... ' are more memorable than any amount of well-intended theory.

**Conclusions**

In this chapter we have:
- defined autonomy in speaking.
- looked at ways that opportunities for self-regulation in the skill of speaking can be provided both in the classroom and outside it.
- discussed why tasks should be productive, purposeful, interactive, challenging, safe, and authentic.

Classroom speaking activities that require a degree of autonomy include:
- giving presentations and talks
- telling stories, jokes, and anecdotes
- drama activities, including role-plays and simulations
- discussions and debates
- conversation and chat

Feedback on such activities needs to be handled sensitively so as to respect the learners' need to experience autonomy, but, at the same time, to provide a useful feedback loop for the improvement of subsequent performance. Feedback that is offered as 'repair' may be less inhibiting than overt correction.

Finally, we looked at ways learners can take responsibility for developing their speaking skills outside the classroom, including the use of taped dialogues, computer-mediated communication, and reflective journals and portfolios.

**Looking ahead**

The last three chapters have dealt with discrete aspects of the skill of speaking, and specifically those classroom activities that target awareness, appropriation, and autonomy. In the next chapter we will look at:
- how speaking can be integrated into a teaching programme.
- how speaking can be assessed.

# 7 Planning and assessing speaking

- Integrating speaking into the curriculum
- Organizing a speaking syllabus
- Classroom talk
- Assessing speaking
- Assessment criteria

**Integrating speaking into the curriculum**

In designing and implementing a language course, how much emphasis should be given to speaking? How will this emphasis vary according to such factors as the level of the learners and their learning context? Should speaking be taught separately or integrated into the teaching of other aspects of linguistic competence? And what is the role of the coursebook and other materials in teaching speaking? Finally, how can speaking be assessed? These are some of the issues that will be reviewed in this final chapter.

## Weighting

The relative weighting of skills work in a course will depend to a large degree on the learners' needs. Learners studying in an ESL context (that is, learning English as a second language in order to integrate into an English-speaking culture) will probably be highly motivated to improve their speaking skills as quickly as possible. Eva, a Polish emigrant to Canada, describes how she felt insufficiently prepared for speaking in her ESL classes:

> Practice is the best thing to learn. When we were by [i.e. at] the school we were in a lot of contact with English, but when I had to go out to work and speak the language, I was so scared. You don't have the practice, just the structures.

Learners studying in an EFL context (i.e. learning English as a foreign language) and in their home culture are not likely to feel as much urgency, although speaking may be a priority in the long term. Learners whose purpose is more academic (EAP, i.e. for attending a university course in an English-speaking country) may need to concentrate more on written language than on spoken. Learners who are learning English as an international language (EIL), and who therefore will be communicating primarily with other non-native speakers, are more likely to prioritize intelligibility over accuracy, especially with regard to pronunciation. And the speaking skills a business person will require are likely to differ markedly from those that are needed by a tourist – the former needing to be competent in a wider variety of genres and registers.

## Needs analysis

This suggests that, without a clear assessment of learners' needs, the relative weighting assigned to different skills will be difficult to judge. Likewise, the learners' needs will also determine the best balance between accuracy and fluency. Analysing learners' needs can be done informally, simply by talking to them, or, more formally, through the use of questionnaires or by interviewing training managers or other stakeholders. If, for example, a group of learners has requested a tailor-made course to improve their workplace English use, the following questions would need to be addressed to the individuals in the group:

1 How often do you use English at work?
   - all the time
   - frequently
   - occasionally
   - very rarely
2 How much of your workplace English is spoken (rather than written)?
   - all
   - most
   - some
   - none
3 Is your spoken English face to face or over the phone/Internet?
   - face to face only
   - phone/Internet only
   - both face to face and on the phone/Internet
4 Do you speak with native or non-native speakers in English?
   - native speakers only
   - non-native speakers only
   - both native and non-native speakers
5 Is your spoken English mainly
   - social?
   - technical?
   - both social and technical?
   - other? (please specify)
6 Is your spoken English mainly
   - formal?
   - informal?
   - both formal and informal?
7 Do you speak English mainly
   - with one other person?
   - in groups?
   - both with one person and in groups?
8 Do you speak English mainly
   - with the same person or people all the time?
   - with different people all the time?
   - with both the same people and with different people?

Further questions of a more diagnostic nature, such as those relating to the problems that the candidates may have experienced in their use of English, could then be asked. The use of simulations and role-plays to identify learners' needs and problems is also an option, albeit a fairly labour-intensive one.

Of course, it is seldom, if ever, the case that a group of learners will have identical needs, and the design and running of a course will need to be able to accommodate diversity in this respect. Some initial discussion with the class about their needs and preferences can help to make this diversity explicit and form the basis for some kind of negotiation. Using the format of a consensus debate (see page 103), for example, the learners can at first individually, and then as a group, rate the following statements:

> I/We would like to do a lot of speaking and listening.
> I/We would like to do a lot of reading and writing.
> I/We would like to do a lot of grammar.
> I/We prefer speaking in pairs and groups.
> I/We prefer speaking in open class.
> I/We would like to do discussions and debates.
> I/We would like to do role-plays and drama.
> I/We would like to give presentations to the class.
> etc.

These preferences can be renegotiated periodically throughout the course and can also serve as the basis of the post-course evaluation.

### Placement tests

At the very least, a **placement test** should be used for an initial assessment of the candidates' speaking skills. This applies equally to learners whose needs are very specific and to those whose needs are only vaguely formulated. It should be obvious that a quick paper-and-pencil test, such as a grammar multiple choice test, is totally inadequate in terms of assessing a learner's speaking ability. Nor is a formal interview necessarily the best way of assessing speaking if the candidate's workplace English involves informal interaction in groups. In the absence of a clear specification of needs, a placement test of speaking should include a range of interaction types. The following, for example, should serve for most general purposes, and need not last longer then ten to fifteen minutes:

1 A short informal chat, initiated by the interviewer.
2 The candidate chooses a topic from a list, or a picture from a selection, and talks for a minute or so about it. Or a picture story could serve as the basis for a narrating task.
3 The interviewer asks further questions about the topic.
4 The candidate is then invited to ask the interviewer some questions, e.g. about the institution, course of study etc.

Criteria for assessing the candidate's oral ability will be discussed below, but it is important to regard the test as a test of speaking, not solely of grammatical accuracy.

## Balancing accuracy and fluency

Implicit in the kinds of decisions that need to be made at the planning stage is the issue of how to find the right balance between accuracy and fluency. At issue is not just a question of weighting, but of order. Should, for example, a focus on accuracy precede a focus on fluency, or should it come later? For a long time, language teaching operated on the basis that accuracy should precede fluency and that the only speaking that learners were allowed was the oral manipulation of recently taught grammar structures. Teaching sequences were based on the initial mastery of such items (known as **discrete items** of grammar). Only later were these items combined with other, previously learned items, and practised in free production. A great deal of remedial teaching was also required, since accuracy was as much the goal as the starting point of this very form-focused approach. And the standard by which accuracy was judged was based on descriptions of written, rather than spoken, language. In fact, language learners were set objectives that most native speakers would find hard to meet. The philosophy is summed up in this comment by Louis Alexander, from an introduction to a course published in 1967:

> The student should be trained to learn by making as few mistakes as possible. He should never be required to do anything which is beyond his capacity.

A literal interpretation of such a view led to the almost indefinite postponement of fluency practice altogether. The following 'Letter to the Student' from the fourth level of a general English course for secondary school students represents an extreme example of this attitude:

> Dear Pupil:
> You have now reached the stage in your studies that you have been dreaming about ever since you started studying English: you are going to TALK! How many times have you asked yourself when, oh, when will your teacher let you talk? You wanted to talk from your first lesson – and you did talk from your first lesson by answering questions – but your teacher kept interrupting you by correcting and directing your answers. You said over and over again that you wanted to talk, why didn't your teacher let you! The answer is simple: you were not ready yet …

Quite understandably, this 'delayed production' approach to language learning frustrated many learners. Moreover, it did not reflect either the way the first language is acquired or the way that second languages are learned naturally. In these cases, speaking precedes, rather than follows from, complete mastery of the linguistic system. In fact, in the case of many L2 learners, complete mastery may be an unrealistic goal. It may be sufficient simply to achieve the ability to communicate intelligibly across a limited range of genres, contexts, and topics. In other words, fluency may be a more important objective than formal accuracy.

A radical re-thinking of the relative importance of accuracy and fluency fuelled the evolution of the **communicative approach**. Learners who needed to achieve a functional degree of communicative competence as soon as possible were becoming impatient with the accuracy-fixated approach. Moreover, research was showing that learning processes, whether of language or of any cognitive skill, involve cycles of trial, error, and re-trial, and that precision is late acquired. Accordingly, proponents of a more fluency-driven approach proposed a model of instruction that started out from (rather than ended up with) the learner's attempts to communicate. The traditional and communicative models of instruction are contrasted in the following diagram:

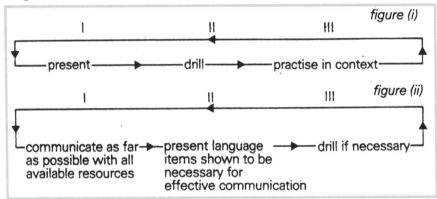

One manifestation of this communicative model of instruction was task-based learning (see page 119). But even teachers who adhered to the traditional model find it hard to resist this new prioritizing of fluency. A more tolerant attitude to error has been one effect. Another has been the increased incorporation of fluency activities into the classroom, even at relatively early levels. This recognition of the importance of speaking for its own sake – not simply as proof of grammar mastery – has radically affected course design, including syllabus specifications and assessment.

**Organizing a speaking syllabus**

It has been a constant theme in this book that the skill of speaking is much more than the oral production of grammar or vocabulary items. It follows that a syllabus that is only or largely a list of such items is not a speaking syllabus. As well as re-focusing attention on fluency, the advent of the communicative approach has given rise to what are called multi-layered syllabuses, which specify not only the grammar and vocabulary components, but also the skills to be taught. Here, for example, is part of the speaking component of a recently published general English course at intermediate level, extracted from the contents page:

| in unit one ... | in unit two ... | in unit three ... |
|---|---|---|
| speaking | speaking | speaking |
| • talk about conversation topics | • talk about travelling | • describe your perfect day |
| • talk about jobs | • discuss different forms of transport | • describe a famous actor |
| • discuss hopes and plans | • decide what makes a good holiday | • talk about your childhood |
| • start a conversation with a stranger | • how to ... make a complaint | • talk about your interest in the arts |
| • how to ... keep a conversation going | | • how to .... talk about your past |

Also available are materials that specifically target aspects of the speaking skill, such as conversation, discussion, and oral presentations. Here, for example, is the contents page for a book on teaching conversation, in which the material is organized in terms of specific conversational microskills and a selection of conversational topics:

**Part 1: Conversation Skills**
Unit 1 Conversation and cooperation
Unit 2 Expanding what you say
Unit 3 Supporting what you say
Unit 4 Summarising to show understanding
Unit 5 Going back to an earlier point
Unit 6 Vague language

**Part 2: Conversation Topics**
Introduction
Unit 1 Talking about children
Unit 2 Talking about etiquette
Unit 3 Talking about toys and games
Unit 4 Talking about a special occasion
Unit 5 Talking about age
Unit 6 Talking about marriage
Unit 7 Talking about friends
Unit 8 Talking about superstitions

Other ways of organizing the content of a speaking syllabus include the following:

* **spoken grammar**, including heads, tails, ellipsis, discourse markers etc.
* **pronunciation features**, including stress and intonation, rhythm, and chunking
* **communication strategies**, such as paraphrasing, appealing for help, formulaic language etc.
* **conversational routines or gambits**, such as openings, closings, interrupting, changing topic etc.

- **conversational rules and structure**, such as turn-taking, adjacency pairs, and the co-operative principle
- **speech acts**, such as inviting, requesting, complimenting etc.
- **registers**, such as formal vs informal language
- **scripts**, such as service encounters, greetings, telephone language
- **genres**, such as telling stories and jokes, making a speech, interviews
- **situations**, such as at a ticket office, at the bank, in a restaurant etc.
- **cultural factors**, such as politeness, taboo topics, use of gesture etc.

A speaking course that aimed to be comprehensive might choose from all the above strands, taking into account the specific needs and abilities of the learners.

### Integrating skills

A separate speaking syllabus, or a stand-alone speaking course, might give the impression that speaking exists in isolation. In fact, very few speech events in the real world exist independently of other language skills. Even such relatively non-interactive speech events as making a formal speech involve some preparation in the form of writing. And of course speaking always assumes a listener, whether physically present or at the other end of the line. Indeed, one of the chief difficulties that speakers of another language face is the problem of understanding what other speakers are saying. Eva, the Polish migrant who we quoted at the beginning of this chapter, had this to say about her first job in Canada:

> [Munchies] was the first place that I had to be able to communicate in English. I was having a hard time with understanding, speaking, and making conversation with somebody. Many times we were having a break together and they were talking about something. Sometimes I didn't understand the topic and many times if I did understand, I didn't know enough correct words to take part in conversation …

Speaking, therefore, needs to be practised in conjunction with other skills, which suggests an **integrated skills approach**. Nor is listening the only other skill that is implicated. Many real-world tasks that involve speaking may also involve reading and writing as well. A learner's first contacts in an English-speaking country, for instance, may be at the immigration desk of an international airport, where they will not only have to respond to questions, but they will have to interpret and complete an immigration card, follow signs, make a customs declaration, and read the associated literature. Clearly, preparation in the form solely of the speaking dimension of this task would be inadequate.

Moreover, any one speech event is likely to involve a variety of different registers. A business meeting, for example, might start with small talk as participants arrive and take their seats, move into a more formal stage where the chairperson performs various introductory rituals, before breaking into discussion and argument, which may also include banter and word play. At the same time, there will be documents to read, notes to be taken, and possibly some kind of multimedia presentation to observe.

In preparing learners for this kind of integrated experience, integrated tasks will need to complement the more segregated approach favoured by traditional **discrete-item** syllabuses. The need for such an integrated approach is one argument in favour of a task-based syllabus.

## A task-based approach

Earlier in this chapter we outlined a model of instruction based on the learners' attempts to communicate using their available resources. And in Chapter 4 (page 59) we referred to the use of task cycles that follow a 'perform – observe – re-perform' progression. An approach that foregrounds the performance of a task, and which only afterwards focuses attention on the linguistic components of that task, is known as a task-based approach. It contrasts with the approach that is known as PPP (presentation – practice – production), in which the task is the culmination of an instructional sequence rather than its starting-point. Task-based instruction was originally motivated by the belief that a language is best learned through using it, rather than learned *and then* used. As Dave Willis puts it, 'A task-based methodology is based on the belief that out of fluency comes accuracy, and that learning is prompted and refined by the need to communicate.'

The merits of task-based learning in terms of overall language acquisition are still disputed. But as a model for the development of a specific *skill*, it has a lot of attractions. As we saw in Chapter 4, the fluid performance of other skills, such as horse-riding or playing a musical instrument, involves what is essentially task-based instruction. That is, the learner performs successive trials and re-trials, with ongoing assistance from a 'better other', during which features of the new skill are noticed and integrated (or appropriated) into the performer's existing competence. Detailed explanations in advance of the students 'having a go' are often counterproductive.

A task-based syllabus for speaking, then, would be based around a sequence of integrated tasks. These would involve speaking, of course, although not necessarily exclusively. They would also, ideally, reflect the kind of language tasks that the learners would meet in the real world – as identified through needs analysis, for example. In the absence of a clear idea of the learners' future needs, as in the case of a class of teenagers, for example, the tasks should at least aim to cover a representative spread of task types and topics. Generic task types include:

- **surveys** – as when groups of learners collaboratively produce a questionnaire on the subject of music tastes, survey the rest of the class, collate the results, and report on them to the class.
- **design tasks** – as when learners collaborate in deciding on the most effective use for a vacant space in their neighbourhood and present their case to the rest of the class.
- **research tasks** – as when learners use the resources of the Internet, for example, to research an aspect of local history with a view to writing the wording for a new monument.
- **imaginative tasks** – as when learners script, perform, and record a radio drama based on a regional folk tale.

Topic domains can radiate out from the immediate world of the learner, through their local world, to national and global concerns, as in the diagram on the right:

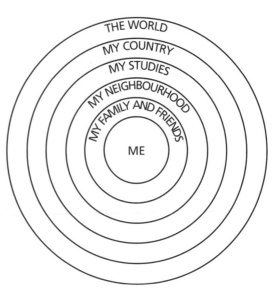

Below, for example, is a syllabus of tasks designed for secondary school students studying English in Spain. The activities are sequenced around the preparation and presentation of a design-type task, whose topic domain is 'the world'. The different language functions involved in the performance of each task are listed in the right-hand column:

| | | |
|---|---|---|
| **3  A GOOD CAUSE** <br> 20 | To design a charity campaign, present it to your classmates and decide which charity you are going to support. | Talking about problems: *The poor are often hungry.* *There is too much dirty water. There aren't enough doctors.* <br> Talking about obligation: *The homeless have to sleep in the streets.* <br> Making suggestions: *We think 'Save the Panda' should get £2,000.* |
| **4  HEROES** <br> 26 | To tell your classmates about your hero and decide who is the 'hero of heroes'. | Talking about personality: *I think Joan of Arc was very brave.* <br> Talking about achievements: *I've discovered a new virus.* *Einstein won the Nobel prize.* <br> Asking/Talking about the past: *Who sang 'Imagine'?* *He lived in Paris.* |

As an example of how a task integrates a variety of skills, including speaking, here is a breakdown of the steps involved in Task 3 of the above syllabus ('A good cause'):

- reading brochures from a variety of charities (*reading*)
- using dictionaries to check the meaning of unknown words (*reading*)
- talking in open class about local charities and discussing their merits (*speaking*)
- working in groups to choose 'a good cause' to prepare a campaign for (*speaking*)
- using dictionaries to access relevant vocabulary (*reading*)
- collaboratively writing the text of a campaign brochure (*speaking and writing*)
- presenting the campaign to the rest of the class (*speaking*)
- listening to and evaluating other groups' presentations (*listening*)
- deciding, in groups, on how a fixed sum of money might most deservedly be allocated between the various campaigns (*speaking*)
- reporting the group decision to the class (*speaking*)

Notice that, not only are there frequent opportunities in this sequence for speaking, but the speaking takes many forms. At times it is informal, unrehearsed, and non-public, as when the groups are talking together to plan their writing. At other times it is more formal, rehearsed, and public, as when the groups present their campaign to the class. An integrated, task-based approach, therefore, would seem to offer plentiful and varied opportunities to develop the speaking skill.

## A genre-based approach

Task-based instruction has been criticized, however, on the grounds that it prioritizes the **processes** of using language, at the expense of a focus on the **products**, i.e. the kinds of texts – both spoken and written – that learners will need to (re-)produce. This is particularly the case in ESL contexts, where learners are under considerable pressure to match their uses of language with the expectations of the target community. A new arrival in Australia, for example, needs to know how to make a good impression in a job interview, taking into account the way that such interviews are typically transacted in the Australian context. A task-based approach, it is argued, favours an implicit approach to instruction, when in fact learners need clear and explicit models of the language behaviours they are going to encounter.

A genre-based approach attempts to redress this lack of explicitness by providing direct instruction in the way language events such as job interviews are typically realized, and by relating these features to the social context and purpose of the event. In Chapter 2, we defined a spoken genre as simply being 'a type of speech event' such as a chat, an interview, or a presentation. Proponents of a genre-based approach would go further and emphasize that genres are not only structured in predictable ways, but that they are purposeful, socially situated, and culturally sanctioned. The starting point in a genre-oriented sequence of instruction, therefore, is establishing the social purpose and cultural context of the genre in question. This is followed by the presentation and analysis of a typical example before learners attempt to create their own examples. The more elaborated description of the teaching/learning cycle of a genre-oriented approach at the top of page 122 comes from Susan Beez's *Text-based Syllabus Design*.

This lesson sequence is then mapped on to a syllabus that is designed to reflect the practical needs of learners as they integrate into the target culture. In the middle of page 122, for example, is an excerpt from the contents page of an intermediate course for ESL learners in Australia. It shows the topical and speaking/listening strands of the course.

The task-based versus genre-based distinction echoes the process versus product approaches to the teaching of writing (see *How to Teach Writing* by Jeremy Harmer in this series). The same criticisms of a product-based writing can be levelled at genre-based teaching. That is, the focus on imitating models does not necessarily reflect the way that writers (and speakers) produce texts (or talk) in reality. Moreover, the emphasis on the genre as a culturally instituted form obscures the fact that successful language users are able to use their knowledge of genres creatively in order to achieve their own purposes. Also, in emphasizing cultural factors, a focus on genre tends to

| First stage of the cycle | • activities build knowledge of a context of language use which is related to learner needs<br>• activities involve visuals, realia, excursions, discussions, field-work, and vocabulary building<br>• parallel activities build cross-cultural strategies and pronunciation or spelling skills |
|---|---|
| Second stage of the cycle | • involves a close investigation of the purpose and structure of a model of a text type which occurs in the context<br>• students focus on the register and language features which are central to the text achieving its purpose<br>• language features are studied at both whole text and clause level |
| Third stage of the cycle | • initial activities provide students with opportunities to use the text type with support<br>• later activities gradually demand more independent performances |

| Unit | Topics | Speaking and Listening |
|---|---|---|
| 1 | • family and neighbours | • listening to a casual conversation<br>• starting conversations<br>• changing topics in conversation |
| 2 | • early childhood services<br>• immunisation<br>• travelling and sight-seeing | • talking to an early childhood nurse<br>• giving instructions<br>• giving personal information<br>• checking personal information |
| 3 | • conflict<br>• smoking<br>• opinions<br>• attitudes<br>• marriage customs | • listening to a casual conversation<br>• expressing anger<br>• closing a conversation |

exaggerate the differences between the way language events are achieved in different cultures, at the expense of the similarities. Finally, by foregrounding the analysis of texts, there is a danger that teaching can become somewhat academic, with a preponderance of 'chalk-and-talk' type instruction.

Nevertheless, for certain learners in particular contexts, a genre-based approach may be more efficient. More formulaic genres, such as formal presentations, lend themselves to a genre-based approach. And the emphasis on context, purpose, and the expectations of the audience, foregrounds the importance of taking register factors into account (see page 19).

In the end, it is not that difficult to marry the two approaches, the task-based one and the genre-based one. This can be done either by including a more explicit focus on the features of the genre in a task-based approach or by beginning a genre-based approach with a 'trial run'. This then can be used as a point of comparison with the performance of a more expert user.

**Classroom talk**  Whatever the instructional approach that is adopted, the single most influential factor in the development of speaking skills is probably the classroom culture. A classroom culture that prioritizes communication is bound to promote the development of speaking, especially if the quality of communication is high. Herbert Puchta and Michael Schratz define this kind of communication in these terms:

> If the participants are being both frank and considerate, independent yet co-operative, and are speaking willingly and comprehensibly to particular listeners about things that matter to them both, then the quality of communication is high.

This requires, in turn, that teachers accept that – for at least some of the time – learners should have some say (literally) in the classroom culture. The writer Claire Kramsch offers some ground rules whereby more say can be devolved to the learners, through, for example, allowing them topic control and giving them more responsibility for the turn-taking in classroom talk. Here are some of her 'rules' for teachers:

- use the target language not only to deal with the subject matter but also to regulate the interaction in the classroom. You will thus offer a model of how to use interactional gambits in natural discourse.
- keep the number of display questions (i.e. teacher questions that are aimed at getting learners to 'display' their knowledge, such as 'What's the past of go?') to a minimum. The more genuine the requests for information, the more natural the discourse.
- build the topic at hand together with the students; assume that whatever they say contributes to the topic. Do not cut off arbitrarily a student's utterance because you perceive it to be irrelevant. It might be very relevant to the student's perception of the topic.
- tolerate silences; refrain from filling the gaps between turns. This will put pressure on students to initiate turns.
- encourage students to sustain their speech beyond one or two sentences and to take longer turns; do not use a student's short utterance as a springboard for your own lengthy turn.
- extend your exchanges with individual students to include clarification of the speaker's intentions and a negotiation of meanings; do not cut off too soon an exchange to pass on to another student.
- pay attention to the message of students' utterances rather than to the form in which they are cast. Keep your comments for later.
- make extensive use of natural feedback ('hmm'/'interesting'/'I thought so too') rather than evaluating and judging every student utterance following its delivery ('fine'/'good'). Do not over-praise.
- give students explicit credit by quoting them ('just as X said'); do not take credit for what students contributed by giving the impression that you had thought about it before.

There is a growing body of opinion that the kind of classroom culture implied by the above 'rules' not only promotes speaking skills but also serves in the development of the language overall, including its grammar and vocabulary. That is, that through talk, a language can be acquired. The idea is, of course, not new. Here, for example, is how the writer of a textbook for Argentinian students put it, in 1953:

> Conversation must not only be considered one of the aims of an English course. It is the means to the desired end. Only by speaking a language can we ever hope to learn it.

This view contrasts radically with the 'don't talk until you are ready' philosophy mentioned earlier in this chapter. In fact, there has always been an uneasy tension between these two extremes: the view that using a language follows on from the learning of it and the view that using *is* learning. Making room for conversation in the classroom, and giving learners more say in the classroom culture, is often compromised by the belief that learners need grammar first and foremost. This can result in situations where learners are sometimes actually discouraged from speaking about the things that they want to, as in this extract from a classroom in Mexico. (The numbers in brackets represent pause length in seconds.)

> [after taking the register, the teacher starts chatting to students]
> T: Well then, Jorge ... did you have a good weekend?
> S: Yes
> T: What did you do?
> S: I got married.
> T: [smiling] you got married. (0.7) You certainly had a good weekend then. (5.0) [laughter and buzz of conversation]
> T: Now turn to page 56 in your books. (1.6) you remember last time we were talking about biographies ... .
> [T checks book and lesson plan while other students talk to Jorge in Spanish about his nuptials.]

This kind of situation, in which the textbook and lesson plan conspire against the development of an authentically communicative classroom culture, is often exacerbated by the nature of many tests and examinations – a subject which we will now turn to.

**Assessing speaking**

Testing, both informally and formally, takes place at the beginning and at the end of most language courses, as well as at various times during the course itself. We have already noted that, at placement, an assessment of learners' speaking skills can be done by means of an interview that includes different oral tasks. A placement test that includes no spoken component provides an inadequate basis for assessing speaking, and the same can be said for any test of overall language proficiency, whether it aims to test **progress** during the course, or **achievement** at the end of it.

The problem, however, with including an oral component in a test is that it considerably complicates the testing procedure, both in terms of its practicality and the way assessment criteria can be reliably applied. Setting and marking a written test of grammar is relatively easy and time-efficient. A test of speaking, on the other hand, is not. If all the students of a class have to be interviewed individually, the disruption caused, and the time taken, may seem to outweigh the benefits. Moreover, different testers may have very different criteria for judging speaking, differences that are less acute when it comes to judging writing or grammar knowledge, for example.

All these difficulties aside, a language programme that prioritizes speaking but doesn't test it *through* speaking can't be said to be doing its job properly. To re-state a point made earlier: a test of grammar is *not* a test of speaking. The need to test speaking through speaking is particularly acute if learners are hoping to enter for a public examination which includes a speaking component, such as the Cambridge First Certificate in English (FCE) or the International English Language Testing Service (IELTS) examination. Furthermore, where teachers or students are reluctant to engage in much classroom speaking, the effect of an oral component in the final examination can be a powerful incentive to 'do more speaking' in class. This is known as the **washback effect** of testing, i.e. the oral nature of the test 'washes back' into the coursework that precedes it.

It therefore makes sense to incorporate oral testing procedures into language courses despite the difficulties. Since the activities designed to test speaking are generally the same as the kinds of activities designed to practise speaking, there need be no disruption to classroom practice. The challenge is more in deciding and applying satisfactory assessment criteria.

### Types of spoken tests

The most commonly used spoken test types are these:

- **Interviews** – these are relatively easy to set up, especially if there is a room apart from the classroom where learners can be interviewed. The class can be set some writing or reading task (or even the written component of the examination) while individuals are called out, one by one, for their interview. Such interviews are not without their problems, though. The rather formal nature of interviews (whether the interviewer is the learner's teacher or an outside examiner) means that the situation is hardly conducive to testing more informal, conversational speaking styles. Not surprisingly, students often underperform in interview-type conditions. It is also difficult to eliminate the effects of the interviewer – his or her questioning style, for example – on the interviewee's performance. Finally, if the interviewer is also the assessor, it may be difficult to maintain the flow of the talk while at the same time making objective judgments about the interviewee's speaking ability. Nevertheless, there are ways of circumventing some of these problems. A casual chat at the beginning can help put candidates at their ease. The use of pictures or a pre-selected topic as a focus for the interview can help, especially if candidates are given one or two minutes to prepare themselves in advance. If the questions are the same for each interview, the interviewer effect is at least the same for all candidates. And having a third party present to co-assess the candidate can help ensure a degree of objectivity.

- **Live monologues** – the candidates prepare and present a short talk on a pre-selected topic. This eliminates the interviewer effect and provides evidence of the candidates' ability to handle an extended turn, which is not always possible in interviews. If other students take the role of the audience, a question-and-answer stage can be included, which will provide some evidence of the speaker's ability to speak interactively and spontaneously. But giving a talk or presentation is only really a valid test if these are skills that learners are likely to need, e.g. if their purpose for learning English is business, law, or education.

- **Recorded monologues** – these are perhaps less stressful than a more public performance and, for informal testing, they are also more practicable in a way that live monologues are not. Learners can take turns to record themselves talking about a favourite sport or pastime, for example, in a room adjacent to the classroom, with minimal disruption to the lesson. The advantage of recorded tests is that the assessment can be done after the event, and results can be 'triangulated' – that is, other examiners can rate the recording and their ratings can be compared to ensure standardization.

- **Role-plays** – most students will be used to doing at least simple role-plays in class, so the same format can be used for testing. The other 'role' can be played either by the tester or another student, but again, the influence of the interlocutor is hard to control. The role-play should not require sophisticated performance skills or a lot of imagination. Situations grounded in everyday reality are best. They might involve using data that has been provided in advance. For example, students could use the information in a travel brochure to make a booking at a travel agency. This kind of test is particularly valid if it closely matches the learners' needs. One problem, though, with basing the test around written data is that it then becomes a partial test of reading skills as well.

- **Collaborative tasks and discussions** – these are similar to role-plays except that the learners are not required to assume a role but simply to be themselves. For example, two candidates might be set the task of choosing between a selection of job applicants on the basis of their CVs. Or the learners simply respond with their own opinions to a set of statements relevant to a theme. Of course, as with role-plays, the performance of one candidate is likely to affect that of the others, but at least the learners' interactive skills can be observed in circumstances that closely approximate real-life language use.

### The CELS Test of Speaking

In practice, formal examinations often include a range of test types, so that the strengths of one type counterbalance the weaknesses of another and allow learners to show themselves to their best advantage. For example, the Cambridge Certificate in English Language Speaking Skills (CELS) Test of Speaking, like its Trinity College equivalent, the ESOL Spoken Grade Examinations, is a stand-alone test of speaking that can be taken at three different levels. It involves a number of different interactions. The standard format for the test involves two examiners and two candidates and lasts 20 minutes. One examiner acts as both assessor and interlocutor (that is to say, he or she interacts with the candidate at the same time as evaluating the candidate's responses), while the other acts as assessor only. The format of the test is as follows:

- The candidates are given the first task (see Example 1 on page 128) and have a minute and a half to prepare.
- The candidates talk individually with the interlocutor on prompts they have chosen and in response to questions from the interlocutor. This stage lasts seven minutes.
- They are then given the second, interactive, task (see Example 2 on page 128), and, again, have a minute and a half to prepare.
- The candidates talk together for four minutes, using the written stimulus.
- Then there is a three-way discussion related to the task between the candidates and the interlocutor, which lasts another four minutes.

Note that the test involves individual speech, dialogue, and three-way discussion. Note also that the tasks require only the most minimal processing of written text, to ensure that reading ability does not interfere with the testing of speaking.

**Assessment criteria**

Having obtained a sample of the learner's speaking ability, how does one go about assessing it? There are two main ways: either giving it a single score on the basis of an overall impression (called **holistic scoring**) or giving a separate score for different aspects of the task (**analytic scoring**). Holistic scoring (e.g. giving an overall mark out of, say, 20) has the advantage of being quicker, and is probably adequate for informal testing of progress. Ideally, though, more than one scorer should be enlisted, and any significant differences in scoring should be discussed and a joint score negotiated.

Analytic scoring takes longer, but compels testers to take a variety of factors into account and, if these factors are well chosen, is probably both fairer and more reliable. One disadvantage is that the scorer may be distracted by all the categories and lose sight of the overall picture – a woods-and-trees situation. Four or five categories seems to be the maximum that even trained scorers can handle at one time.

For the CELS Test of Speaking (described above) there are four categories: 'Grammar and Vocabulary', 'Discourse Management', 'Pronunciation', and 'Interactive Communication'. They are described in the following terms:

- **Grammar and Vocabulary** – on this scale, candidates are awarded marks for the accurate and appropriate use of syntactic forms and vocabulary in order to meet the task requirements at each level. The range and appropriate use of vocabulary are also assessed here.
- **Discourse Management** – on this scale, examiners are looking for evidence of the candidate's ability to express ideas and opinions in coherent, connected speech. The CELS tasks require candidates to construct sentences and produce utterances (extended as appropriate) in order to

CANDIDATE'S TASK SHEET
Preliminary, Part 1

Example 1

You are going to talk about the town or city where you are now. What do you like or dislike about it?

The following may give you some ideas.

Choose 2 or 3 that you would like to talk about. Add other ideas of your own if you wish. Think about what you want to say and make some notes if you want.

- Restaurants
- Buildings
- Cinemas, clubs etc
- Shops
- Traffic problems
- Parks or gardens
- Other …

CANDIDATE'S TASK SHEET
Preliminary, Part 2

Example 2

The school or college where you learn English is planning a new Students' Room for all the students to use. Below are some ideas for things to put in the Students' Room.

Look at the list of suggestions below and decide which three you think are best. Add other ideas of your own if you wish. Think about what you want to say, and make some notes if you want.

- Food and drink machines
- TV
- Computers with Internet
- Magazines and newspapers
- Comfortable furniture
- Table tennis
- Other things

Discuss your choices with your partner and try to agree on three things which you think would be most popular with the students.

Then the examiner will ask you about your discussion.

When do you think you would use a room like this?

convey information and to express or justify opinions. The candidate's ability to maintain a coherent flow of language with an appropriate range of linguistic resources over several utterances is assessed here.

- **Pronunciation** – this refers to the candidate's ability to produce comprehensible utterances to fulfil the task requirements, i.e. it refers to the production of individual sounds, the appropriate linking of words, and the use of stress and intonation to convey the intended meaning. L1 accents are acceptable provided communication is not impeded.

* **Interactive Communication** – this refers to the candidate's ability to interact with the interlocutor and the other candidate by initiating and responding appropriately and at the required speed and rhythm to fulfil the task requirements. It includes the ability to use functional language and strategies to maintain or repair interaction, e.g. in conversational turn-taking, and a willingness to develop the conversation and move the task towards a conclusion. Candidates should be able to maintain the coherence of the discussion and may, if necessary, ask the interlocutor or the other candidate for clarification.

It is worth emphasizing that grammatical accuracy is only one of several factors, and teachers need to remind themselves when assessing speaking that even native speakers produce non-grammatical forms in fast, unmonitored speech. It would be unfair, therefore, to expect a higher degree of precision in learners than native speakers are capable of.

The CELS Test of Speaking can be taken at three levels, which correspond to levels B1, B2, and C1 of the Common European Framework (CEF). The CEF provides useful descriptors for different skills competences at each of its six levels, and these in turn can provide teachers with handy criteria for assessing their learners' abilities. The CEF distinguishes between *speaking* (or *oral production*), on the one hand, and *spoken interaction* on the other. The descriptors for oral production at all levels are displayed in the table below, in the form of 'can do' statements.

|  | OVERALL ORAL PRODUCTION |
|---|---|
| C2 | Can produce clear, smoothly flowing well-structured speech with an effective logical structure which helps the recipient to notice and remember significant points. |
| C1 | Can give clear, detailed descriptions and presentations on complex subjects, integrating sub-themes, developing particular points and rounding off with an appropriate conclusion. |
| B2 | Can give clear, systematically developed descriptions and presentations, with appropriate highlighting of significant points and relevant supporting detail. Can give clear, detailed descriptions and presentations on a wide range of subjects related to his/her field of interest, expanding and supporting ideas with subsidiary points and relevant examples. |
| B1 | Can reasonably fluently sustain a straightforward description of one of a variety of subjects within his/her field of interest, presenting it as a linear sequence of points. |
| A2 | Can give a simple description or presentation of people, living or working conditions, daily routines, likes/dislikes etc as a short series of simple phrases and sentences linked into a list. |
| A1 | Can produce simple mainly isolated phrases about people and places. |

Descriptors for spoken interaction (as opposed to one-way oral production) include such factors as:

- turn-taking skills
- communication strategies
- spontaneity
- asking for clarification
- information exchange
- politeness strategies

Finally, learners themselves should be encouraged to take some responsibility for their own assessment. Asking them to record and assess themselves, using criteria that have been discussed in advance, is one way of doing this. Simply counting the length of pause-free runs is a crude but effective way of measuring their fluency, especially over successive repetitions of the same task. Here, for example, is a student doing a task once and then five minutes later, having given it some thought. The pauses are marked with vertical lines.

> **First attempt:**
> I remember my worst teacher | um still. | Er he was very very bad because | er, the time that I | was | er learning | with | him | er was compliba ... | complicate | to me understand | er all the lesson | because | because | he | was | not | expressive. | Er he | only | only | speak | explained | the | the lessons | er always following the | the | the book | without | to | explain more things | about | er the lesson | or about | the thing that | can | be important to | to | to understand the | the lesson

> **Second attempt:**
> I still remember my | last | my | my worst teacher because | er he was really | really bad. | It was | very complicate to understand | him | because | he wasn't | too much expressive | and | and he was really | really really serious. | Mm-hm mm he | only | followed | the | the | the book | doing the lesson | without to explain | more important things | so | we | we didn't understand the | the | the main matter of the | of the lesson

In the first attempt the student averages 2.1 words per run; in the second this has improved to 2.4. A less laborious way of measuring fluency might simply be to count the runs of three words or more: nine in the first instance, twelve in the second.

Learners can also be asked to evaluate their speaking using the kinds of 'can do' statements included in the CEF (see above). As more and more coursebooks incorporate CEF assessment guidelines, these are likely to become a familiar tool in both the planning and testing of speaking activities.

**Conclusions**   In this chapter we have considered ways that speaking can be integrated into the curriculum, including issues of:

- **weighting** – different learning objectives (such as business, travel, academic studies) will determine the priority given to oral communication.
- **syllabus organization**, in terms of:
  - speech genres, e.g. small talk, meetings, presentations
  - situations, e.g. at the post office, in the pub
  - topics
  - conversational skills, strategies, and rules
  - speech acts, such as requesting, apologizing
  - conversational routines
  - spoken grammar, vocabulary
  - pronunciation.
- **methodological approach**, e.g.:
  - a task-based approach, where the *processes* of speaking are foregrounded
  - a genre-based approach, where the *products* of speaking are foregrounded
  - a classroom culture that prioritizes authentic communication.
- **testing** – including the choice of test-type (interview, role-play etc) and scoring criteria (e.g. holistic or analytic).

**Postscript**   The point has been made, but is worth repeating by way of a conclusion, that the teaching of speaking depends on there being a classroom culture of speaking. Learners cannot learn to speak simply through doing reading and writing activities, or exercises on vocabulary and grammar. Where speaking is a priority, language classrooms need to become *talking* classrooms. The point is well made in this extract from a short story about a language school in New Zealand, where one of the students has been rushed into hospital. The teacher and students visit the hospital. Afterwards they return to the classroom:

> … now any semblance of instruction had broken down.
>
> Or had it? What does a teacher do at a language school?
>
> You talk, essentially. You need some kind of crutch – a textbook, a theme – but the main thing is to talk and cause the students to talk. There are the ESOL dogmas: the Four Skills – two *active* (Speaking, Writing), two *passive* (Listening, Reading); the Three 'P's – Presentation, Practice, Performance. Essentially, though, it's talking that's required.
>
> We talked that day …

# Task File

## Introduction

- The exercises in this section all relate to topics discussed in the chapter to which the exercises refer. Some expect definite answers, while others only ask for the reader's ideas and opinions.
- Tutors can decide when it is appropriate to use the tasks in this section. Readers on their own can work on the tasks at any stage in their reading of the book.
- An answer key is provided after the Task File (on pages 146–150) for those tasks where it is possible to provide specific or suggested answers. The symbol ☞ beside an exercise indicates that answers are given for that exercise in the answer key.
- The material in the Task File can be photocopied for use in limited circumstances. Please see the note on the inside front cover for photocopying restrictions.

## TASK FILE Chapter 1

# What speakers do

### A  Speech production  Page 1

Here is an extract of naturally occurring speech from *Advanced Conversational English* by Crystal and Davy. What features (such as filled pauses) are evidence of its real-time, spontaneous production?

**A:** you know as I came back to London and er then I discovered how how lovely Maida Vale is

**B:** it's a beautiful area mm

**A:** I can see trees from my window and Walking walking to Sainsburys is lovely because there's there's there's some flats and there there's lots of lawn and then trees and some lovely old houses on the other side of the road and it really – in the autumn I mean – the leaves and everything

**B:** yes

**A:** it looks really lovely and it's a very wide road too – there are wide roads everywhere there – it's not like where we lived in London before – it was dirtier and smokier

### B  Turn-taking  Page 8

Here is an extract of talk taken from earlier in the Kedgeree conversation. Can you find examples of:

- overlapping turns
- simultaneous utterances
- incomplete turns
- repeated turns
- backchannelling
- topic shift

> Transcription conventions:
> =   contiguous utterances, i.e. ones that run on without pause, despite interruptions from other speakers
> |   overlapping utterances
> ||  simultaneous utterances
> ( )  a slip

(21)  Simon: It's cows' stomachs. It's what makes cheese set.
(22)  Nick:   Renin?
(23)  Kath:   Yes.
(24)  Simon: So why      | vegetarian Jewish women eat cheese
(25)  Nick:             | It's rennet isn't it =
(26)  Kath:   || so you make it with =
(27)  Hilda:  || Scott? [offering something]
(28)  Kath:   = I can't remember actually remember what junket is, it's as though it's a sort of | horrible =
(29)  Simon:    | Rennet and milk
(30)  Kath:   = horrible form of blancmange =
(31)  Scott:  || Junket?
(32)  Nick:   || What's rennet?
(33)  Scott:  Junket?
(34)  Hilda:  || Rennet? It's what makes it curdle
(35)  Simon: || It's milk
(36)  Nick:   I would imagine junket to be (blen) blended offal
(37)  Scott:  No [laughs] not at all

(38)  Kath:  || It's milk pudding
(39)  Hilda:  || No it is actually, yes | that's
(40)  Simon:                              | that's where rennet comes from =
(41)  Scott:  Oh?
(42)  Simon: = it's actually very small | [unclear]
(43)  Scott:                              | but I mean it's like a yoghurt

## TASK FILE Chapter 2

# What speakers know

### ✐ A   Speech genres   Page 13

Classify the following speech genres according to the criteria in the table. (The first one has been done for you).

|  | purpose | participation | planning |
|---|---|---|---|
| **airport announcements** | transactional | non-interactive | planned |
| **university lecture** |  |  |  |
| **telephoning a friend** |  |  |  |
| **radio interview** |  |  |  |
| **TV weather forecast** |  |  |  |
| **asking street directions** |  |  |  |
| **speech of thanks** |  |  |  |

### ✐ B   Spoken grammar and vocabulary   Page 20

The following extract from the play *Tea Party*, by Harold Pinter, attempts to replicate spoken language. How successful is it, do you think? What features of spoken grammar and vocabulary does it display, and which ones are missing?

**John:**   (*choosing a cake*) These are good.
**Tom:**   What are they?
**Diana:**   (*choosing a bridge roll*) These look nice.
**Lois:**   You look wonderful, Mrs Disson. Absolutely wonderful. Doesn't she, Peter?
**Disley:**   Marvellous.
**Lois:**   What do you think of your grandsons?
**Father:**   They've grown up, haven't they?
**Lois:**   Of course, we knew them when they were that high, didn't we, Tom?
**Father:**   So did we.
**Tom:**   Yes.
**Willy:**   Big lads now, aren't they, these two?
**John:**   Cake, Granny.
**Mother:** No, I've had one.
**John:**   Have two.
**Father:**   I'll have one.
**Mother:** He's had one.
**Father:**   I'll have two.

### ✐ C   Spoken narratives   Page 14

Here is an example of authentic spoken narrative, taken from *The Language of Conversation* by F. Pridham. Compare it with the Kedgeree story on page 2. What features do they have in common? To what extent do you think these two narratives are representative of their genre?

**Richard:** I'll tell you one thing when we moved to London and we'd been here for about a month and we were just driving around looking at the sights and we were driving past Buckingham Palace right and Chloe's in the back of the car right this is so funny um and she said there it is there's Buckingham Palace woah woah oh we should open the window oh and the Queen lives there oh look the flag's up the Queen's in there now and she said is that the Queen's house then? and we said yeah she said ooh fancy building a palace next to the main road

**Raj, R & J:** (*laughter*)

**Judy:** on the main road (*laughs*) which is logical

**Richard:** which is very observant absolutely why did they do that she said and actually I couldn't think because the road was probably there when they built it although there wouldn't have been cars on it

**Raj:** I hope you praised her for making a good point

**Richard:** well we fell apart

# Speaking in another language

**A    Communication strategies**    Page 29
Identify the communication strategies that learners are using in these extracts. (For a list, see page 29.)

1  The flat is very cold because it no have calefaction. [for *heating*].
2  It's make glass for put flower inside. You put flower in it. Water and then some flower. On table. [for *vase*]
3  I want some of those things, you know, like … [sings first bars of *Happy Birthday* and pretends to blow out candles]. [for *candles*]
4  **T:**  Yumiko, what would you take with you?
    **S:**  Erm, my family photo.
    **T:**  You'd take your family photos?
    **S:**  Yes, erm, my photo book. [for *photo album*]
5  … and then the truck hit the cyclist and he fall down and the man call the the the *ambulancia*. [for *ambulance*]
6  I want a ticket with ten, erm, things. [for *journeys*]

**B    Word frequency**    Page 34
Here are the 30 most frequent words in written and spoken English respectively (according to the CANCODE corpus, as listed in *Vocabulary: Description, Acquisition and Pedagogy* by McCarthy and Carter). What significant differences do you note, and how might you account for these differences?

|    | Written | Spoken |    | Written | Spoken |
|----|---------|--------|----|---------|--------|
| 1  | the     | the    | 16 | you     | no     |
| 2  | to      | I      | 17 | but     | oh     |
| 3  | of      | you    | 18 | at      | so     |
| 4  | a       | and    | 19 | his     | but    |
| 5  | and     | to     | 20 | as      | on     |
| 6  | in      | it     | 21 | be      | they   |
| 7  | I       | a      | 22 | my      | well   |
| 8  | was     | yeah   | 23 | have    | what   |
| 9  | for     | that   | 24 | from    | yes    |
| 10 | that    | of     | 25 | had     | have   |
| 11 | it      | in     | 26 | by      | we     |
| 12 | on      | was    | 27 | me      | he     |
| 13 | he      | is     | 28 | her     | do     |
| 14 | is      | it's   | 29 | they    | got    |
| 15 | with    | know   | 30 | not     | that's |

## TASK FILE
## Chapter
## 4

# Awareness-raising activities

✎ **A**　**Awareness-raising**　Page 41
Here are some coursebook activities whose aim is to raise awareness about different features of speaking. Can you identify the focus of each activity?

---

**1**

**2** Read this news story and underline the words you think the speaker will stress.

Hijackers are still holding twenty-three passengers in a plane at Manchester airport. They hijacked the flight from London to Glasgow last Thursday. The hostages have now been sitting in the plane without food or water for three days.

▣ **Listen and check. Read the news story aloud.**

---

**2**

How important is small talk when you do business? Look at the table. Then think about the situation in your country and another country you know well.

| | UK | Finland |
|---|---|---|
| When do people make small talk? | before a meeting | after a meeting |
| How important is small talk? | important | not very important |
| What do people like talking about? | people they both know; places they both know; hobbies; the weather; the cost of living | people they both know; places they both know; sports; the countryside; the cost of living |
| What don't people talk about very much? | their salaries; their families; food | their salaries; the weather; political opinions |

---

# English in use

**3**

1　✳ **Against the clock!** You have three minutes to list the expressions in the box under one of the three headings.

　　Agreeing　Disagreeing　Half agreeing

**Pronunciation**

1　Predict the intonation patterns of expressions 1 to 10 in *Against the clock!*

2　▣3 Listen and check.

3　Listen again and repeat.

| | |
|---|---|
| 1　You're absolutely right. | 8　That's rubbish! |
| 2　I don't think that's true. | 9　I see what you mean, but … |
| 3　I disagree, I'm afraid. | 10　That's true in a way, but … |
| 4　I take your point, but … | 11　That's right. |
| 5　Absolutely. | 12　Well, it depends. |
| 6　Come on! | 13　To a certain extent, but … |
| 7　Do you really think so? | 14　I would agree with that. |

2　Which two expressions would you probably only use with people you know well?

---

　　**PHOTOCOPIABLE**

**4** 🔊 **31** Ann is saying goodbye to Bob after an evening at his house. Read the conversation and complete the 'goodbye' expressions using the words in the box. Then listen and check your answers.

**4**

| you | better | after | having | be | regards | been | already | must | for |
|-----|--------|-------|--------|-----|---------|------|---------|------|-----|
| Give | Take | Bye | journey | See | will | | | | |

# The long goodbye

**Ann:** I'd (1) _____ be going.

**Bob:** It's (2) _____ lovely to see you.

**Ann:** Thank you for (3) _____ me.

**Bob:** Thanks (4) _____ coming.

**Ann:** I'll (5) _____ off then.

**Bob:** Give my (6) _____ to your family.

**Ann:** I (7) _____ .

**Bob:** (8) _____ me a ring.

**Ann:** Okay. I really (9) _____ be off now.

**Bob:** (10) _____ it easy.

**Ann:** (11) _____ you.

**Bob:** Look (12) _____ yourself.

**Ann:** (13) _____ for now.

**Bob:** Safe (14) _____ .

**Ann:** Love (15) _____ .

**Bob:** Missing you (16) _____ .

**7 Read the following sentences. Who said them?**

**5**

1 And the holidays are good as well. Mind you, I need them after a twelve week term, I can tell you.
2 I reckon that drivers who are born here have it much easier when they take the exam, that's my honest opinion.
3 I should have been looking around for something better, but you know, it's difficult when you've got a family and so on.
4 OK, there are always days when you think, there must be an easier way of earning a living, you know, when you've had a particularly difficult class, or a pupil has been rude to you.
5 I mean, things are a bit tight, no holidays, no meals out, that sort of thing.
6 Well, the city council has a kind of office that looks after the taxi drivers, gives them licences, and all that.

**8 When we speak, we often say things which we don't usually write. Look at the sentences in activity 7 again. Cross out anything which we would not usually write.**

**TASK FILE**
**Chapter**
**5**

# Appropriation activities

**A** **Dialogues** Page 72

Create a 10–12-line dialogue that includes a number of different speech acts (see page 51 for an example). Draw a flow chart of the dialogue (see page 75 for an example). How could you use this flow chart in the classroom?

**B** **Communicative activities** Page 79

Here are some speaking tasks that have a built-in communicative element. To what extent are they in fact really communicative? (See page 80 for some of the features of communicative activities.)

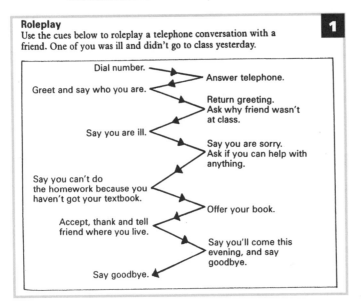

**Roleplay** **1**
Use the cues below to roleplay a telephone conversation with a friend. One of you was ill and didn't go to class yesterday.

Dial number. → Answer telephone.

Greet and say who you are. → Return greeting. Ask why friend wasn't at class.

Say you are ill. → Say you are sorry. Ask if you can help with anything.

Say you can't do the homework because you haven't got your textbook. → Offer your book.

Accept, thank and tell friend where you live. → Say you'll come this evening, and say goodbye.

Say goodbye.

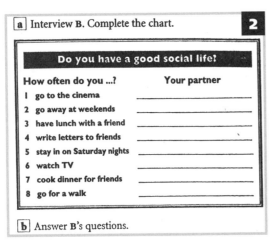

**2** **a** Interview **B**. Complete the chart.

**Do you have a good social life?**

| How often do you ...? | Your partner |
| --- | --- |
| 1 go to the cinema | |
| 2 go away at weekends | |
| 3 have lunch with a friend | |
| 4 write letters to friends | |
| 5 stay in on Saturday nights | |
| 6 watch TV | |
| 7 cook dinner for friends | |
| 8 go for a walk | |

**b** Answer **B**'s questions.

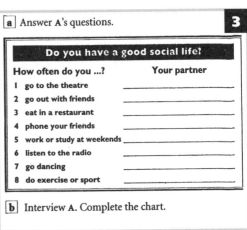

**3** **a** Answer **A**'s questions.

**Do you have a good social life?**

| How often do you ...? | Your partner |
| --- | --- |
| 1 go to the theatre | |
| 2 go out with friends | |
| 3 eat in a restaurant | |
| 4 phone your friends | |
| 5 work or study at weekends | |
| 6 listen to the radio | |
| 7 go dancing | |
| 8 do exercise or sport | |

**b** Interview **A**. Complete the chart.

## Unit 12 (Exercise 3b), page 115)

STUDENT B

Look at the things in the photographs. You and your partner have different things. Take it in turns to describe them. Don't say the names. Your partner should guess what they are. Examples:
*It's / They're made of ... It's / They're for ... It's / They're round / square ...*

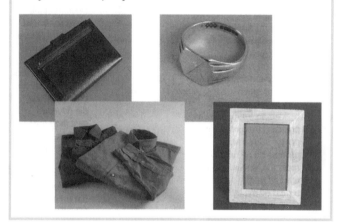

## Unit 12 (Exercise 3b), page 115)

STUDENT A

Look at the things in the photographs. You and your partner have different things. Take it in turns to describe them. Don't say the names. Your partner should guess what they are. Examples:
*It's / They're made of ... It's / They're for ... It's / They're round / square ...*

## TASK FILE
## Chapter
## 6
# Towards autonomy

🔑 **A** **Criteria for speaking tasks** Page 90
Evaluate the following speaking tasks in terms of these factors:
- productivity
- purposefulness
- interactivity
- authenticity

---

**4** Work in a group with other **1**
students and discuss whether you
agree or disagree with the
following statements. Give
reasons.

1 Exams are not an accurate
  measure of a person's ability.
2 A mixture of exams and
  coursework is a good idea.
3 You should repeat a school
  year if you fail your exams.
4 You should be told the
  questions a little time before
  you go into the exam.
5 Exams should involve an oral
  and a written part.
6 Competitive exams are a good
  idea.

---

## Role-play **2**

1 *A* You're going to be interviewed for one of
these jobs. Think about what you'll say.

Wanted: **NANNY** to look after three young children.
Some cooking and cleaning. Driver's licence
essential.

Wanted: **ENGLISH TEACHER** to teach beginners.
Training given, but experience an advantage.

Wanted: **ACTORS/ACTRESSES** for small parts in a
popular daytime soap. Good acting ability essential.

*B* You're about to interview A. Think of
some questions you will ask him/her.

Now conduct the interview.

---

## Get talking **3**

9 **In groups, choose two places in your country
to enter the 'City/Region of the Year'
competition.**

1 Think about climate, people, countryside, food
  and drink, prices, free-time activities and
  culture.

2 Decide which place should win:
  First Prize _____
  Second Prize _____

3 Tell the class which city/region won the
  competition and why.

---

## Speak out **4**
### Are you a typical woman or man?

1 Think of five ways that you're typical and five ways that you're not.
Think about these things.

**topics of conversation**
**books and magazines**
**working** **TV**
eating socializing
clothes and hair

**In groups.** Compare your ideas. Who is most 'typical', and who is
most 'different'?

---

**B    Dealing with error**    Page 91

Comment on the effectiveness of the way the teacher deals with error in each of these (genuine) examples of classroom interaction, taken from *Introducing Classroom Interaction* by Amy Tsui:

**1**

**T:** What did they do after their wonderful meal? What did they do after their wonderful meal? What did they do after their wonderful meal? Chi Hang.

**S:** They told stories and sing songs by the –

**T:** Sing song? Pay attention. Once again. Not sing song, past tense please.

**S:** They told story and sung song.

**T:** Sung? No.

**S:** Sang song.

**T:** Once again.

**S:** They told story and sing song.

**T:** No.

**S:** They told story and sang song by the fire.

**T:** They told story and sang song by the fire.

**2**

**T:** What is the lesson in this story? What did you learn from the story? Anyone who can tell me?

**S:** Care to choose the friend.

**T:** Steven, repeat your answer again loudly.

**S:** Mm, choose someone's friend more carefully.

**T:** Choose someone's friend more carefully. How? How should you be careful? What kind of friend should you choose?

**S:** Careful and friendly.

**T:** Careful?

**S:** Helpful.

**T:** Helpful? Helpful. Right. Helpful and friendly.

# Planning and assessing speaking

**TASK FILE
Chapter
7**

✏ **A    Accuracy and fluency**    Page 115

Read these extracts from the teacher's book introductions to some ELT courses. Where does each one seem to position itself in terms of the relative weighting and ordering of accuracy and fluency?

1   Students are encouraged to communicate orally from the beginning, using the limited language at their disposal to its full effect … . When new structures are introduced, meaning is established and controlled practice is given to ensure that production of form and pronunciation is as accurate as possible. Gradually, students are encouraged to use new vocabulary and structures more freely and to incorporate them into their general pool of productive language. (from *The Beginners' Choice* by Mohamed, S and Acklam, R)

2   By Upper-Intermediate, most SS [students] have attained a reasonably good level of oral fluency … however, SS tend to have many ingrained, often basic, errors of grammar and pronunciation which need to be eradicated. Make it clear from the outset that the main aim of the course is also to help SS communicate more *accurately*. … For example, the GET IT RIGHT activities that precede conversation exercises help to alert SS' attention to a particular problem area before they speak. (from *English File Upper Intermediate* by Oxenden, C and Latham-Koenig, C)

3   The approach is based on the belief that attention to grammatical structure is essential in language learning, but it does not assume that grammar should therefore be the *starting point* of learning. The direction, therefore, is from fluency to accuracy … **Language Activities** contain activities in which learners are encouraged to communicate their own ideas. At the same time, these activities are designed to create a need for the language points covered in each unit. (from *Highlight Pre-Intermediate* by Thornbury, S)

4   *Framework* creates an environment in which students can express themselves orally on topics of genuine and contemporary interest. The great majority of tasks give them the opportunity to speak both before the task (warmers) as well as during and after its completion (follow-up discussion or role-plays). Targeted lexical and grammatical structures are also practised orally. These tasks work by transforming language input into personalised communication which matters to the students – there is always a reason to speak. (from *Framework, 2* by Goldstein, B)

✏ **B    Assessing conversation**    Page 127

On page 129 are the Common European Framework descriptors for Oral Production, displayed in the six bands from A1 to C2 , i.e. from beginner to advanced. Here are some of the descriptors for Conversation. Can you match them with their band?

| C2 | 1. Can participate in short conversations in routine contexts on topics of interest. |
|----|--------------------------------------------------------------------------------------|
| C1 | 2. Can converse comfortably and appropriately, unhampered by any linguistic limitations in conducting a full social and personal life. |
| B2 | 3. Can maintain a conversation or discussion but may sometimes be difficult to follow when trying to say exactly what he/she would like to. |
| B1 | 4. Can make an introduction and use basic greeting and leave-taking expressions. |
| A2 | 5. Can use language flexibly and effectively for social purposes, including emotional, allusive, and joking usage. |
| A1 | 6. Can engage in extended conversation on most general topics in a clearly participatory fashion, even in a noisy environment. |

# Task File Key

## Chapter 1

**A** Features that indicate speech production processes:
- use of pause fillers: *and er then I discovered*
- use of repeats: *there's there's there's some flats …*
- 'add-on' grammar production: *and there there's lots of lawn and then trees and some lovely old houses …*
- vagueness: *there's lots of lawn; the leaves and everything*
- unfinished utterances: *and it really …*
- use of chunks: *really lovely*

**B**
- overlapping turns: e.g. 24 and 25
- simultaneous utterances: e.g. 26 and 27
- incomplete turns: e.g. 24
- repeated turns: 31 and 33
- backchannelling: 41
- topic shift: 27; 28 (where Kath retrieves the topic of, junket)

## Chapter 2

**A**

|  | purpose | participation | planning |
|---|---|---|---|
| **airport announcements** | transactional | non-interactive | planned |
| **university lecture** | transactional | non-interactive | planned |
| **telephoning a friend** | interpersonal | interactive | unplanned |
| **radio interview** | transactional | interactive | (partly?) planned |
| **TV weather forecast** | transactional | non-interactive | (partly?) planned |
| **asking street directions** | transactional | interactive | unplanned |
| **speech of thanks** | interpersonal | non-interactive | planned/unplanned |

**B** Features of spoken grammar and vocabulary:
ellipsis: [*Yes, she looks*] *Marvellous*; [*Would you like some*] *Cake, Granny?*
tails: *Big lads now, aren't they, these two?*
tags: *Big lads now, aren't they, these two?*
deixis: *These are good … ; when they were that high*
appraisal: *Marvellous; Absolutely wonderful*

Characteristic features of spoken language that are not represented are such performance effects as pause fillers, and repeats. Nor are there any instances of vague language. Also there is an absence of discourse markers, apart from the rather formal *of course*.

C At the level of the macro-structure, both stories include these elements, and in the same order:
- an **orientation** to the circumstances of the story, including the setting and characters;
- a **remarkable incident** – in the case of the kedgeree story, this is the complication introduced by Kath's mother; in the Buckingham Palace story it is Chloe's comment about building a palace near the main road;
- a **consequence** of the incident – in Kath's case, her having to sit and watch the others make kedgeree, and in Chloe's story, the fact that the listeners all 'fell apart'.

Also, running through both stories is some form of **evaluation** of the incident, including the drawing of some sort of lesson from each story. In Kath's case she evaluates the situation as *awful*, and afterwards suggests how irrelevant the cooking of kedgeree was. In Chloe's, the speaker says *This is so funny* before telling the story, and then afterwards comments on Chloe's 'logic'.

At the level of grammar and vocabulary, both stories are told in the past, but speech is reported directly. The connector *and* is used to sequence the events, and the chunk 'and she said' is used in both stories. Theatrical devices, such as 'sound effects' (*woah woah*) and mock accents, are also used for humorous effect, a reminder that both stories are designed to amuse the listeners.

The macro-structure and linguistic features are common to most spoken anecdotes, even when the intention is not necessarily to amuse, and therefore can be said to be generic.

## Chapter 3

A The communication strategies used are:
1 foreignizing a word – in this case the Spanish *calefacción* (heating)
2 circumlocution
3 paralinguistics
4 approximation
5 language switch
6 using an all-purpose word

B
- The personal pronouns *I* and *you* are higher up the spoken list, evidence of the interpersonal and interactive nature of a lot of speaking.
- The question responses *yeah*, *yes*, and *no* occur in the spoken list, more evidence of the interactive nature of talk.
- The discourse markers *oh*, *so*, and *well* are more frequent in spoken language, indicating the importance of signalling speaker intention constantly.

- *know* also features in the spoken list, probably mainly as a result of the frequency of the expression *you know*.
- The higher frequency of *do* and *what* is evidence of the greater number of questions in spoken language.

## Chapter 4

**A**

1 sentence stress, i.e. emphasizing the main information-carrying words;
2 cultural knowledge, specifically differences in conversational style;
3 speech act knowledge, specifically ways of expressing agreement and disagreement;
4 conversational closings;
5 discourse markers (*I mean, you know* etc) and vague expressions (*that sort of thing*).

## Chapter 5

**B** Using the criteria outlined in Chapter 4:

**Speaking activity 1:**
- is not motivated to achieve an outcome, other than the completion of the task
- does take place in real time
- does not require participants to listen as well as speak (since both participants can see how the conversation is going to develop)
- the outcome is predictable (for the same reasons)
- in principle, the language is not restricted even though the conversational moves are preordained; however, the prompts are likely to determine many of the language choices

It is only minimally communicative, therefore.

**Speaking activity 2:**
- is not motivated by the need to achieve an outcome, apart from filling in the chart, e.g. the information that is gathered is not put to any use
- takes place in real time
- requires interaction
- is not 100% predictable
- is highly constrained in terms of the language, in terms of the questions, although not of the answers

The activity is, therefore, not wholly communicative, according to the criteria.

**Speaking activity 3:**
- is motivated to achieve an outcome, i.e. guessing the objects
- takes place in real time
- requires participants to listen as well as speak
- is not 100% predictable
- is not restricted, although there are some prompts that have been provided

It is communicative on all counts, therefore.

## Chapter 6

### A

| | Activity 1 | Activity 2 | Activity 3 | Activity 4 |
|---|---|---|---|---|
| productivity | rubric specifies six discussion topics, and learners are told to give reasons, but, in absence of outcome (see below), no guarantee that this will be productive | not very productive, especially since the number of questions is not stipulated; no task repetition built in, e.g. interview several candidates | lots of categories to consider, so likely to be fairly productive | lots of topics to consider, and specification of number of points to be made, all help increase potential for production |
| purposefulness | no outcome, e.g. to find points of agreement, or draw up a 'policy' on exams for the class | no outcome, e.g. choose the best candidate | class presentation provides sense of purpose, especially if presentations are put to the vote | clearly established outcome (who is most 'typical' …) |
| interactivity | because of above, no incentive to interact | because of above, not a lot of interaction | no interaction guaranteed: group work could be just one or two students participating; the presentations don't include a question-and-answer stage | group work doesn't guarantee interaction, although having a decision to make will require students to listen to one another |
| authenticity | rather academic discussion, although the fact that the task comes from an exam preparation book suggests that it may be relevant to learners | a genuine speaking genre, although the choice of jobs may not be relevant | having to reach consensus, and presenting in public are authentic language activities, even if the topic may not be entirely engaging | not a very authentic task, although the personal nature of the topic will help make the task engaging |

## Chapter 7

### A

1 While prominence is given to early communication, the progression is nevertheless one from strict accuracy to fluency.

2 There is a very heavy emphasis on accuracy: this is 'the main aim', and the writers insist on pre-teaching in advance of communication.
3 The direction is from fluency to accuracy, with the former preparing learners for the latter, rather than vice versa.
4 Fluency is prioritized, with plentiful opportunities for freer speaking; grammar is practised orally before being personalized, implying an accuracy-to-fluency direction.

**B**

**1** – A2; **2** – C2; **3** – B1; **4** – A1; **5** – C1; **6** – B2

# Further reading

For further reading on the subject of spoken language, and of teaching speaking, the following books are recommended:

## Spoken language

Cameron, D (2001) *Working with Spoken Discourse*, Sage Publications.
Carter, R and McCarthy, M (1997) *Exploring Spoken English*, Cambridge University Press.
Pridham, F (2001) *The Language of Conversation*, Routledge.

## Teaching speaking

Burns, A and Joyce, H (1997) *Focus on speaking*, Macquarie University: NCELTR.
Bygate, M (1987) *Speaking*, Oxford University Press.
Dörnyei, Z and Thurrell, S (1992) *Conversation and Dialogues in Action*, Prentice-Hall International.
Hughes, R (2002) *Teaching and Researching Speaking*, Longman.
Nolasco, R and Arthur, L (1987) *Conversation*, Oxford University Press.
Willis, J (1996) *A Framework for Task-Based Learning*, Longman.

The following references and notes are arranged by chapter. The relevant page number of the chapter is shown on the left. In cases where the book referred to is listed above, only the author and date are given.

## Chapter 1

2  The conversation about kedgeree is from the author's data.
3  **Conceptualization and formulation:** The sporting gaffes are from http://www.hamletcroft.co.uk/FamousFootballHowlers.doc
5  **Articulation:** see Kelly, G (2000) *How to Teach Pronunciation*, Longman.
   **Self-monitoring and repair:** The example of repair is from the *Longman Grammar of Spoken and Written English*, (1999), page 1062.
6  **Fluency:** Extract from Kuiper, K and Austin, P (1990) 'They're off and racing now: the speech of the New Zealand race caller', in Bell, A and Holmes, J (eds) *New Zealand Ways of Speaking English*, Wellington: Victoria University Press, page 210.
8  Extract from Crystal, D and Davy, D (1975) *Advanced Conversational English*, Longman, page 19.

## Chapter 2

21 **Grammar:** The information at the end of the section comes from the *Longman Grammar of Spoken and Written English*, based on an analysis of a 40-million word database, or **corpus**, of text, both spoken and written, of (North) American and British English.

23 Conversational extract from Aussietalk, a conversation corpus belonging to the University of Technology, Sydney.

24 Study from Liu, D (2003) 'The most frequently used spoken American English idioms: A corpus analysis and its implications', in *TESOL Quarterly*, 37/4.

## Chapter 3

27 The epigraph is from Grace Nichols (1984), *The Fat Black Woman's Poems*, Virago Press.

29 The extract by McQueen, H is from *Tokyo World*, (1991) Heinemann, page 44.
The extract by Iyer, P is from *The Lady and the Monk*, (1992) Black Swan, page 101.

35 **Vocabulary:** The dictionary entry is from the *Longman Dictionary of Contemporary English*, 2003.
The extract is from Gairns, R and Redman, S – data collected for *Natural English*, Oxford University Press.

37 **Phonology:** The extract from the Japanese speaker is from Wennerstrom, A (2001) *The Music of Everyday Speech*, Oxford University Press, page 233.

## Chapter 4

43 The authentic transcript is from Coates, J (2003) *Men Talk*, Blackwell, page 36.

45 The reality show extract is from:
http://www.channel4.com/bigbrother/news/newsstory.jsp?id=4834

46 The two researchers' work is described in *Language Teaching*, January 2002, #19.

58 The extract is from Johnson, K, 'Mistake correction', in *ELT Journal*, 42/2, 1988, page 93.

59 Jane Willis (1996), page 91.
The extract is from Earl Stevick (1989) *Success with Foreign Languages*, Prentice-Hall, page 148.
Lynch, T (2001) 'Seeing what they meant: transcribing as a route to noticing', in *ELT Journal*, 55/2, pages 124–132.

61 The extract is from Mennin, P (2003) 'Rehearsed oral L2 output and reactive focus on form', in *ELT Journal*, 57/2, pages 133–4.

## Chapter 5

68 Payne, JS and Whitney, PJ (2002) 'Developing L2 Oral Proficiency through synchronous CMC: Output, Working memory, and Interlanguage development', in *CALICO Journal*, 20, cited in *Language Teaching*, July 2003, page 210.

70 Mark Powell, in Lewis, M (1997) *Implementing the Lexical Approach,*, LTP, page 156.

71 Edmund White (1997) *The Farewell Symphony*, Chatto & Windus, page 105.

71 The extract about rephrasing is from Tsui, A (1995) *Introducing Classroom Interaction*, Penguin, page 18.

85 The task repetition example is based on material in Gairns and Redman, *Natural English Pre-Intermediate*, Oxford University Press, Unit 7.

**Chapter 6**

89 Schmidt, R and Frota, S (1986) 'Developing basic conversational ability in a second language: A case study of an adult learner of Portuguese', in Day, R (ed.) *Talking to learn: Conversation in Second Language Acquisition*, Newbury House, page 242.

92 The extract is from Mathers, J (1990) 'An investigation into feedback in an L2 classroom', unpublished MA dissertation, Christ Church College, Canterbury, quoted in Seedhouse, P (1997) 'Combining form and meaning', in *ELT Journal*, 51/4, page 342.

94 The key features are from Morita, N (2000) 'Discourse socialization through oral classroom activities in a TESL graduate program, in *TESOL Quarterly*, 34/2, page 302.

95 Sacks, O (1985) *The Man Who Mistook His Wife for a Hat*, Picador Books, page 105.

101 Charlyn Wessels' article is 'From improvisation to publication on an English through Drama course', in *ELT Journal*, 1991, 45/3.

102 **Discussion questions:** Discussion questions for ESL and EFL classrooms are freely available on the Internet. See, for example: http://iteslj.org/questions/

105 Alexander, L (1967) *First Things First: Teacher's Book*, Longman, page viii.
Hatch, E (1978) 'Discourse Analysis', in Hatch, E (ed.) *Second Language Acquisition: A Book of Readings*, Newbury House, page 408.
Bannink, A (2002) 'Negotiating the paradoxes of spontaneous talk', in Kramsch, C (ed.) *Language acquisition and language socialization: ecological perspectives*, Continuum, page 271.

106 Ernst, G (1994) '"Talking circle": Conversation and negotiation in the ESL classroom', in *TESOL Quarterly*, 28/2.

107 **One of us/Some of us:** I am grateful to Mario Rinvolucri for this idea.

108 From Johnson, K (1995) *Understanding Communication in Second Language Classrooms*, Cambridge University Press, pages 24–25.
**Tape diaries:** Ho, K (2003) 'Audiotaped dialogue journals: an alternative form of speaking practice', in *ELT Journal*, 57/3.

109 The chatterbot conversation is from: http://www.zabaware.com/home.html

110 The journal extract is from Norton, B (2000) *Identity and Language Learning*, Longman, page 96.
The European Language Portfolio extract is from: http://www.culture2.coe.int/portfolio/inc.asp?L=E&M=$t/208-1-0-1/main_pages/contents_portfolio.html

## Chapter 7

112 The extract is from Norton, B (2000) *Identity and Language Learning*, Longman, page 136.

115 Alexander, L (1967) *First Things First: Teacher's Book*, Longman, page xii.

The letter is from Spiro, D (nd) *English for the Brazilian Student, Book IV*.

117 The extract from the intermediate level course is from Gairns, R and Redman, S (2002) *Natural English, Intermediate, Student's Book*, Oxford University Press, page 2.

The extract from a book on teaching conversation is from Geddes, M and Sturtridge, G (1994) *Intermediate Conversation*, Prentice-Hall, page 3.

118 The quotation is from Norton, *op cit*, page 63.

119 Willis, D (1990) *The Lexical Syllabus*, Collins ELT, page 128.

122 Beez, S (1998) *Text-based Syllabus Design*, NCELTR, Macquarie University, page 33.

The excerpt from a contents page is from Delaruelle, S (1998) *Beach Street 2, Student's Book*, NSW Adult Migrant English Service.

123 Puchta, H and Schratz, M (1993) *Teaching Teenagers*, Longman, page 3.

Adapted from Kramsch, C (1985) 'Classroom interaction and discourse options', in *Studies in Second Language Acquisition*, 7, pages 169–183.

124 Halbrich, J O (1953) *Toil and chat: Curso elemental del Inglés*, Buenos Aires, page 84.

Cadorath, J and Harris, S (1998) 'Unplanned classroom language and teacher training', in *ELT Journal*, 52/3, page 188.

128 From Cambridge ESOL website: http://www.cambridgeesol.org/exams/cels.htm

129 *Common European Framework of Reference for Languages: learning, teaching, assessment*, Cambridge University Press, 2001.

131 The short story extract is from Jack Ross, 'A strange day at the language school', *Landfall*, 203, Autumn 2002, pages 119–125.

# Index